PRISONER OF HER PAST

PRISONER *of* HER PAST

A SON'S MEMOIR

HOWARD REICH

Northwestern University Press
Evanston, Illinois

Northwestern University Press
www.nupress.northwestern.edu

Printed in the United States of America

10 9 8 7 6 5 4 3 2 1

Library of Congress Cataloging-in-Publication Data

Reich, Howard.
    Prisoner of her past : a son's memoir / Howard Reich. — Northwestern University
Press ed.
    p. cm.
    "First published 2006 by PublicAffairs under the title The First and Final
Nightmare of Sonia Reich: A Son's Memoir."
    Includes bibliographical references and index.
    ISBN 978-0-8101-2795-1 (pbk. : alk. paper)
    1. Reich, Sonia—Mental health. 2. Post-traumatic stress disorder—Patients—
Biography. 3. Holocaust survivors. 4. Jews—Illinois—Skokie. 5. Skokie (Ill.)—
Biography. I. Reich, Howard. First and final nightmare of Sonia Reich. II. Title.
RC552.P67R45 2011
362.196'85210092—dc23
[B]

                                                 2011026716

For Robbie, Aaron, and Amanda Abramovitz—Sonia's future
And for Pam Becker, my wife and dearest friend

Contents

Acknowledgments

THIS BOOK WOULD NOT HAVE BEEN POSSIBLE WITHOUT THE encouragement of uncounted colleagues and friends.

I owe a great debt to Ann Marie Lipinski, James O'Shea, Robert Blau, George Papajohn, Robin Daughtridge, Stacy Sweat, Michael Miner, Bill Parker, Jill Boba, and Mark Hinojosa, *Chicago Tribune* editors who helped shape the newspaper story—"Prisoner of Her Past"—that inspired this book.

I feel privileged to have worked on this project, and others, with *Tribune* photographer Zbigniew Bzdak, a poet of the camera if ever there were one. My translator, Askold Yeremin, helped make our journey into Ukraine a revelation. I deeply appreciate the candor and helpfulness of the people of the city of Dubno, who generously shared their dark stories and astonishing documents.

Pam Becker, my wife, recognized the depth of my mother's crisis long before I did and guided me through it. My sister Barb Reich-Abramovitz, her husband Lou Abramovitz, and their children Robbie, Aaron, and Amanda Abramovitz were more comforting to me than they ever will know.

I thank Peter Osnos of PublicAffairs, who immediately saw the universal dimensions of this story; David Patterson, who proved a keenly astute editor and deeply empathetic colleague; Melissa Raymond, who lavished great energy, skill, and care on the production of this book; and Jennifer Joel, my agent at ICM, who advised me with wisdom, optimism, and grace. Drs. Haim Dasberg, David Rosenberg, and Henry Krystal helped me enormously, explaining the psychic after-effects of childhood trauma.

I'd like to thank my colleagues at Northwestern University Press, which is publishing this paperback edition, including Mike Levine, my astute editor; Rudy Faust, a passionate champion of my work; and Heather Antti, who meticulously shepherded this text.

These memoirs chronicle my early years of growing up with my family as I remember them. All the facts and names are real, with the exception of a few minor figures whose names have been changed (specifically Sarah, Don, Julia, Eva, and Lara).

Finally, I thank my great-aunt Irene Tannen and my Warsaw cousin Leon Slominski. Without them, I never could have discovered my mother's story.

PREFACE

FEBRUARY 15, 2001

THE PHONE WENT OFF LIKE AN ALARM, SHATTERING A DEEP sleep, and even after I fumbled to pull the handset to my ear, I felt as if I were in a dream.

"Mom went running out of the house tonight," my sister said. "Running on the streets, and the police picked her up and brought her to Aunt Sarah's house."

What?

"The police got her, and she's safe now. What are we going to do?"

Since this had to be a nightmare, there was only one thing to do—hang up the phone and slip back into the comfort of sleep.

The next morning, during breakfast, I remembered the phantom conversation and wondered if it could have been real. The very notion that my mother, at age sixty-nine, would flee her house after dark on a frozen Chicago night and run the streets until she was grabbed by the police should have been too absurd to entertain—unless someone was trying to kill her, or she believed someone was. She was a widow who had spent the years since my father's death virtually hiding in the tiny house where I grew up. How did a woman who constantly checked, double-checked, and triple-checked the dead bolts on the doors of her home end up in the back seat of a squad car?

It took one phone call to my Aunt Sarah to discover that my mother indeed had been hurrying through the streets the night before, that the midnight phone call from my sister was real. Moreover, the next evening, back in her own home, my mother began running the streets again, leading the police to pursue her anew.

It would take a year to figure out why. In the interim, my mother revolved through hospital emergency rooms and psychiatric wards, confounding doctors who quickly realized that she was fully alert and aware, even as she regularly insisted—in the thick Eastern European accent she never lost—that someone was promising to "put a bullet in my head."

In the ER, she nimbly answered all the doctors' questions: What's your name? Sonia Reich. Where are you now? Skokie, Illinois. Who's the president of the United States? George Bush, the second one. What's more, she quickly mastered the identities of all the attending physicians and nurses, calling each by name as if she had known them for years. She could rattle off the birth dates of her children and grandchildren, list the phone numbers of the various taxicab services she used, even detail the prices of dozens of items she bought at the grocery store and how much they used to cost in the late 1940s, when she first came to America, after the war.

Yet she also described in detail the threats that the imaginary killers were making. And she insisted that she would not be alive much longer unless the killers were stopped, especially, she said, since no one seemed to be doing anything to help.

Chapter 1

LEAVING GERMANTOWN

IT SEEMED THE WHOLE WORLD WAS CROWDED INTO MY parents' tiny bakery on Christmas Eve, 1958, customers competing for cookies shaped like Santa Claus, pastries resembling angels in flight, and sheet cakes slathered with images of reindeer and mistletoe. As patrons jostled for position, slowly inching toward the counter, they ogled one fantastic concoction after another, asking in German for a chocolate-covered Bavarian torte or a towering Black Forest cake. Occasionally, the customers nearly toppled the store's Christmas tree.

For the voluble German patrons who packed our bakery, the spectacle must have recalled scenes back in Berlin or Munich, a tantalizing re-creation of the Old Country wedged into Chicago's most robust German neighborhood, more than a decade after the end of the war. Roughly 200,000 Germans flourished in this part of town, on Chicago's North Side, not far from Lake Michigan, and sometimes it seemed as if every one of them made his or her way into our bakery.

1

For a four-year-old boy who could not remember having seen so many people in one place before, this was the greatest night of the year—of my life, in fact. Here we were, at the nexus of the universe, which, to my good fortune, happened to be my parents' little German shop, on an urban strip jammed with European beer gardens and Old World dance halls, intimate cafés that served exotic teas, and sprawling import stores that sold sausages of strange shapes and scents. Kuhn's Delicatessen, Schmid Imports, Black Forest Market, Schwaben Stube eatery, Zum Deutschen Eck restaurant—a walk along north Lincoln Avenue, stretching out from the sprawling six corners of the Lincoln-Belmont-Ashland shopping hub, suggested a stroll through a bustling Frankfurt.

During the day, the avenue shook with the clatter of streetcars rolling past our bakery and the din of hundreds of shoppers bobbing into and out of dozens of European retailers. At night, the fabulous boulevard became a light show, the soft haze of yellow street lamps mingling with the orange and green and blue of enormous storefront signs, the strip producing almost as much wattage as the theater marquees that lit up Chicago's Loop, just a few miles away.

Even our little bakery had a powerful sign, a tower of a thousand miniature lightbulbs reaching to the top of the two-story building, twinkling day and night. "Kruse's Bakery," the sign read, carrying the name of the previous owner, whose shop my father and one of his brothers had purchased just a few years before. After dark, as I looked out of my bedroom window in our apartment, directly above the bakery, I marveled at the spectacle of it all, the glow of the store's sign falling onto my bed, the neighborhood generating heat long after almost everyone had gone to sleep.

Our boisterous shop, I understood with great pride, was a bona fide landmark in Little Deutschland, and my parents played the role to the hilt.

"Wie geht es Ihnen?"—How are you?—my mother asked one customer after the next, before fetching the cookies and cakes and breads that my father and his brother had made just hours (and sometimes just moments) before. Standing four feet, eleven inches tall, my mother did not cut an imposing figure behind the shop's counter, but she made up for her small size with her energy. When the store was at its busiest, she darted from the bakery shelves to the cash register to the customers like some kind of tiny windup figure. Every sale—even of a single Kaiser roll or a lone Danish or a couple of chocolate cookies dusted with sprinkles—seemed a significant event to her. If the patrons noticed my mother's red, frostbitten fingers under the bright fluorescent lights that illuminated the pastries and rolls and cupcakes, they didn't say so, usually offering a simple "Danke schön" after she handed over the goods in crisp, white waxed bags.

Occasionally, my father emerged from the vast baking area behind the store's lobby to observe the scene and chat with his clientele. A white apron drawn around his muscular five-foot, six-inch physique, a paper baker's cap tamping down his thick, wavy red hair, he beamed to see so many people clamoring for his work. They had been lured to his store not only by the dazzling sign outside but, more important, by the luscious pastries and breads artfully arranged in the window display, fronting Lincoln Avenue, and glistening under the little spotlights trained on them. The moment customers pushed through the door, they took in the aromas of sweet creams and candied jellies and freshly baked doughs. I can remember breathing in deeply and never wanting to exhale, because that would mean letting go of this heady bouquet.

How the German locals would have reacted if they had been told that the woman serving the food had been, not so long ago, a child in the crosshairs of German machine guns, that the man presiding over the cakes and breads had been dying of typhoid in Buchenwald, is hard to guess.

Though I didn't know it at the time, my parents had gone through great agonies to arrive at this little shop. My father had led a charmed childhood in Sosnowiecz, Poland, where his large family thrived, operating a successful bakery of their own. But in 1942, when my father was twenty, the Nazis took him to a labor camp and, eventually, on a death march to Buchenwald, while the Allies bombed Europe and pushed the Germans into retreat. My father spent more than a year recuperating in Wiesbaden after the war, then came to Chicago in 1949 to meet surviving relatives and start over, making a living as a baker, the only trade he knew.

My mother as a child had flourished in a little town in easternmost Poland, Dubno, spoiled as the first grandchild in an extended family. But they lost everything with the Soviet occupation of Dubno, in 1939, less than three weeks after Germany and the USSR entered a nonaggression pact that divided Poland between them. Two years later, after the

Nazis broke the deal and pushed deeper into Poland, my mother—barely eleven years old—began a four-year journey of running and hiding. She came to America as a sixteen-year-old, never educated beyond the third grade. In Chicago, where she had relatives, she worked for a pittance in candy and clothing factories. Each morning, she spent an hour before work applying various salves to acne-scarred skin, then rode a bus to work, returning to a rented room late at night, a few dollars richer.

She met my father on a blind date. After a tempestuous courtship—my mother once throwing her engagement ring at my father over a disagreement, long since forgotten—they married in 1953 and prepared for the arrival of their first child, me, the next year. My mother was so weak, thin, and ill during her pregnancy that many a time she didn't have the strength to turn the key in the door of their North Side apartment after coming home from shopping, as she would often tell me later. So while my father was at work, she frequently sat on the carpeted stairs of the building's hallway, waiting for a neighbor to help.

Not long after I was born, my parents had saved enough money from my father's work as a baker to buy Kruse's, in partnership with my Uncle Don. But why, after all they had experienced, choose a bakery in the heart of Germantown? Why not somewhere else—anywhere else?

They homed in on one of the busiest commercial centers outside the high-rent Loop and took their hard-won knowledge of German culture and taste with them, hoping to make a buck in the process. In ethnic, blue-collar Chicago, where else would they go? Greektown? Chinatown? If that meant keeping quiet about who they were—Jews in Germantown— in order to survive, that was a price they were willing to pay. Their identity already had cost them so much more. (I thought this through, of course, only years later.)

This was our family's little secret. My father told me we were Jewish, although he did not tell me what this meant, just that I was not to tell a single person. Only my father and mother and me were to know—plus my aunts and uncles and cousins and second cousins and in-laws and their cousins. But no stranger—no one outside the family—must ever find out.

The secret was safe with me. Who cared about an identity I didn't understand anyway? I was growing up in the most sumptuous place on earth, our huge apartment above the bakery seeming to stretch for miles from one end of the building to the other. Every morning, I'd race downstairs directly into the store and pick out that day's breakfast: chocolate cake, honey cake, pound cake, cheesecake, cupcakes, jelly rolls, cinnamon rolls, apple twists, muffins, white bread, black bread, banana bread, cherry bread— every baked good imaginable sat there waiting for me, for the taking, every morning of my young life.

After picking out what I wanted and grabbing a tiny carton of extra pulpy orange juice, I climbed onto a stool behind the counter and savored my meal, watching people pour into the shop on the way to work, the gruff businessmen who grabbed their rolls and coffee and ran, the moms who stocked up a week's worth of goods and got a bit of a discount for it, and the odd man who called himself "Bungo" and insisted he had the telekinetic power to make things move by pointing his finger at them. He proved it by placing a fresh cigarette on the glass countertop above one of the store's cookie displays and wagging his forefinger as the cigarette rolled back and forth. Amazing.

My mother entertained and endured these characters with considerable cheer, joking and laughing with them, thanking them for shopping at our bakery, and urging them to come back soon.

Often, while enjoying breakfast, I studied the enormous front page of the morning's newspaper, trying to read all the words, often zeroing in on the color editorial cartoon, attempting to figure out who those pencil-sketched people were and what they were saying. Then I jumped off the stool and ran into the baking area, where my father and Uncle Don kneaded doughs and lifted enormous pans into ovens, then pulled them out with gigantic pan holders. From early in their workday, large rings of sweat had gathered around the necks of their white T-shirts, around their underarms, and even on the brims of their baker caps. In the summer, I couldn't understand how they endured the heat; in the winter, though, the deep warmth of the place made you feel as though you never could be cold again.

I marveled at how fast my father could make little Kaiser rolls and birdies by hand, several dozen a minute, it seemed, and how perfectly turned each one was. His hands— remarkably large and tough and discolored a pale orange, perhaps from so many years of working large clumps of dough—moved relentlessly, like machines. I watched in awe, too, as Uncle Don—not quite as brawny as my dad but nearly as deft—created wedding cakes, architectural triumphs, one layer delicately positioned atop the next and supported by tiny white pillars, the structure topped by plastic statuettes of the bride and groom in formal attire.

It was obvious to me even then that my father and his brother were men of tremendous skill, even though their stained white work clothes were not as sleek as the three-piece suits that often walked into our store. In a way, these brothers were artists, though, unlike the work of painters or writers, their masterpieces were designed to disappear at the very instant they were being enjoyed.

My father told me he had learned to make these cakes and breads back home, in Poland, where his father taught him the trade. He didn't say why his father and mother and most of his siblings and uncles and aunts weren't alive anymore. Nor did my mother mention what happened to her mother and father and their many sisters and brothers and children, except to note that they all had died some years earlier. I didn't understand why there were so many grandparents on TV and in our store and on the street but none in our life. And I sensed that I was not allowed to ask.

Early every Sunday morning (the only day the bakery was closed), I jumped out from under the covers, sprinted down the long hall to my parents' room and dove into their bed, while they struggled to wake up. They seemed amused as I burrowed between them, and before long my father was playing the "tap-tap" game with me—telegraphing rhythms on my shoulder and challenging me to guess the name of the tune he was performing. I had no idea at that point how much he had wanted to become a professional musician, nor how much talent he had, nor why this never happened.

As far as I was concerned, he already was a great musician. I could tell whenever he picked up his cream-colored Hohner accordion and played waltzes and polkas for me. He told me he bought the instrument in Germany years ago and learned to play it by ear. He was a painter, too, as anyone who walked into our apartment could tell from the art on our walls. My dad's oil renderings of ships at sea and pencil sketches of birds in flight suggested the work of a man with years of formal training, though he was entirely self-taught.

Once we finished playing several rounds of our self-styled version of "Name That Tune," we climbed out of bed, my parents speaking Polish to one another, fast and freely. (I was bewildered as to what they were saying, until I started to crack the code while I was in kindergarten. Though I never said a word in Polish, I learned to understand my parents' secret language nearly as well as they spoke it—or I believed I did.) My mother soon began washing dishes from the night before, and my father started making "matzoh brei," mixing a batter of eggs, cracking and dipping sheets of matzoh into it, and frying the strangely shaped creation in a pan. You could hear the food sizzle on the stove, my father constantly turning the matzoh brei one way or another to make sure it was evenly browned. This weekly breakfast—probably in existence since the Hebrews were booted out of Egypt—was the only palpable sign that anyone in this house was Jewish, for there were no prayer books for Shabbos, no menorahs for Hanukkah, no mezuzah on the door, no *tfillin* or yarmulkes or Stars of David. At least none that I remember.

In the late afternoons, we watched Leonard Bernstein's *Young People's Concerts* on TV, my dad softly whistling along to a Schubert symphony or a melody by Brahms, while I lay on the couch and reveled in the radiant sound of the New York Philharmonic, led by that hyperkinetic man on the podium. Or my dad fixated on the *Fight of the Week*, swinging his clenched fists as the battles unfolded in the ring, my mother urging him to calm down.

Before the fighters were completely bloodied, my mother took me for my bath, a pleasant experience until she got to my hair. After lathering it up, she began scratching so hard and for so long—digging her fingers deep into my scalp— that it seemed as if she were trying to scrape something off of me. It hurt.

Often, we spent Sundays visiting aunts and uncles, my dad fixing a clip-on bow tie to my pressed white shirt and telling me, with a huge smile on his face, "You look like a million dollars." Then he helped my mother pick the best dress to wear and the right costume jewelry to match it, meticulously combing her hair for her and, finally, proudly settling my mother and me into our two-toned green Chrysler sedan.

Come Monday, it was time for school. A babysitter picked me up in the morning and brought me home afterward. Not for one moment was I to be left unattended, my parents said—I must always be holding the hand of a grown-up. I must never play with friends unless a trusted adult was close by, and the moment I returned home from school, I must come inside and stay there. Alone upstairs above the bakery after school, I amused myself for hours writing little stories or drawing pictures or watching Gene Autry or *The Honeymooners* on TV—yet I yearned for a friend or a sibling or someone, anyone, to talk to, to play with.

By the time I arrived at school each day, I was starved for contact with other kids and found it impossible to sit in my seat for more than a few moments. Instead, I roamed the classroom—even as the teacher spoke—making appointments with friends to play with me during recess. No matter how many times I was ordered back to my seat, I quickly bounced up again, working the room.

Finally, when we were handed our first-grade report cards, I was dismayed to learn I had earned all U's—for "unsatisfactory," the equivalent of today's F for "failure." A perfect record.

I dreaded bringing home the report card and showing it to my parents, but since it had to be signed, there was no choice. The shop was full of customers as my mother called my father out from the baking area. He pulled the blue paper out of the small manila envelope, read it, and turned white with anger. Still clad in his pale, stained baking uniform, he sat down on a chair behind the counter—the same counter where I always ate my breakfast—and said, "Come over here."

I knew this was going to be bad.

"Come over here," he repeated.

"No, you're going to hit me."

"Come over here—I won't do anything."

I made the mistake of believing him, he grabbed me when I was within arm's reach, put me over his knee, and delivered the fiercest beating I had ever experienced, right there in the bakery, with all the customers watching.

But I learned my lessons: Never believe what your parents tell you, and never tell them the truth.

Not long after, I committed some other transgression upstairs in our apartment, my dad told me to "come over here," and I immediately ran, taking off like a fugitive, our last major encounter playing in my memory. My father chased me around the dining room table, finally cornering me, until I backed into a metal radiator, split the back of my head, and saw blood pouring onto the floor. Hair never again grew from that spot on my scalp.

On that Christmas Eve, 1958, my Aunt Julia came to the bakery to pick me up and take me to see Santa Claus at Goldblatt's department store down the street. She arrived exactly when she said she would, zipped me into my winter coat, and pulled a hat down over my ears, then walked me into Goldblatt's so that I could tell Santa what I wanted for Christmas.

But when we reached the store, we saw that the waiting line for Santa was staggeringly long, wending its way through aisle after aisle. It would take hours before we could get within striking range.

My aunt, however, had a plan: she whispered into my ear that when she gave me the signal, I was to follow her instantly, no questions asked—we were going to cut in line ahead of everybody, saving ourselves hours of waiting. At the moment my aunt saw her opening, she yanked my arm and I scurried right along and suddenly found myself standing near the front of the line.

I hadn't known my aunt could be so crafty. It would be decades before I realized she had been applying survival skills honed in Poland, during harsher times.

It was the tallest, most ominous building I had ever seen, covering half a city block and reaching several stories high, its narrow green spire culminating in a mighty cross that nearly disappeared into the sky.

I could see St. Alphonsus Church from a mile away, and the closer we came to it, the more frightening and majestic it always seemed. Just to get into the place one had to climb seventeen stone steps, an Everest for a kid my age. Then I would try to pull open the massive oak doors—or someone dragged them open for us—and we stepped into near-darkness, until my eyes adjusted to the faint glow of candle-light. Once they did, the room seemed like none on earth, but a heaven or hell, sixteen stone columns holding up an immense vaulted ceiling, dozens and dozens of pews stretching out in front of us, as far as I could see.

My babysitter—a short, slightly bent German woman in her seventies wearing a babushka and a loose-fitting old dress—walked me here from our bakery every afternoon after school for weekday Mass. My parents had told me that she was my new grandma, that I should do whatever she told me and follow her wherever she wanted to go. So I did, as she held my hand and we marched toward the altar at St. Alphonsus. While we walked, Grandma pointed out the huge and terrifying tableaus carved in stone on the walls, each depicting a scene in the crucifixion of Jesus, each with a script that I could not read placed below.

"Jesus is condemned to death," Grandma read the first panel to me. She spoke only German, which I quickly was picking up by spending so much time with her. "Jesus is made to bear His Cross," read the second tableau, showing a bearded man nearly crushed under the weight of an enormous cross.

As the story progressed, the pictures got worse. "Jesus falls the third time," showing helmeted Romans and a mob whipping and beating Him. Then, "Jesus is stripped of His garments," "Jesus is nailed to the cross," and "Jesus dies on the Cross."

I paid close attention to these gruesome images, while Grandma instructed me to do whatever she did, to pray when she prayed, kneel when she knelt. She told me that Jesus Christ was the Lord, that every child must learn to accept this truth, that I must believe or I would be damned to hell.

I believed, I believed. How could anybody do otherwise? I learned to kneel, to cross myself, to light a candle—with Grandma's help—and to otherwise try to be a good Catholic boy. As best as I could figure out, I was Jewish—whatever that meant—when I woke up in the morning, Catholic in the afternoon, and some combination of each late at night. I had never seen the inside or, as far as I know, the outside of a synagogue.

Above all, though, I was becoming German, if only because Grandma—or Oma, as I called her in German—spoke not a word of English. Before long, I was translating for her in grocery stores and speaking Deutsch as fluently as English—better, maybe, since I was spending more time with my babysitter than with any other adult.

"Yes, that's the right price for six bottles of 7-Up," I would tell Oma in German after the cashier at the little A&P grocery store in our neighborhood rang up a charge that Grandma didn't like. "She just wasn't sure about the price," I would assure the cashier in English.

One afternoon, after Grandma returned me to the bakery, I found myself annoyed at something my father did or said and—in an act of open rebellion—yelled at him "Du bist verrückt," meaning "You are crazy."

To my shock, my father didn't lunge at me this time but, rather, tried to suppress a smile, as did my mother (less successfully), at the discovery that their son spoke German. They seemed to delight in this, my mother and father and I from this point forth speaking the language of the neighborhood to one another.

Nevertheless, my parents eventually would dismiss Oma, after I tripped over a stool in the apartment above the bakery, splitting my forehead while in her care. As the blood gushed from my scalp, my mother screamed out "Robert, Robert!" to my father back in the bakery, and he came running upstairs, picked me up, and carried me to the doctor's office, a few doors down Lincoln Avenue. I had never felt safer than in that moment, in his sturdy broad arms, and though my head throbbed with pain, I felt no fear, my father's massive physical strength clearly capable of protecting me and my mother from anything in this world.

In fact, the palms of his outsized hands seemed to contain some kind of mysterious healing power. By now, at age five, I had long since developed the debilitating headaches that I later would learn were migraines, and the half tablet of orange-flavored St. Joseph aspirin that my parents gave me made no dent in them. So whenever the pain struck, my father put me to bed and placed one hand or the other on my forehead, to make the hurt go away. When his hands rested on my head, my pain began to subside.

My mother tried her healing powers on my migraines once or twice, too, but, alas, her tiny, beet-red palms and bony, narrow fingers never had the same effect. I felt badly to tell my mother that only dad's hands worked, but as I was in pain, I didn't spare her feelings.

If Christmas Eve was the greatest night of the year at the bakery, all the Saturday nights were a series of close seconds.

My Uncle Don and his wife, Aunt Eva, and their kids would rush into our apartment so that the adults could count the money and organize the books. The grown-ups convened around our huge dining room table, which soon was covered with piles of cash broken down into ones, fives, tens, twenties, and fifties, as well as a sea of coins—pennies, nickels, dimes, quarters, and fifty-cent pieces—spilling everywhere. My father and uncle calculated the week's take, my aunt wrote down the figures, and my mother worked quietly in the kitchen, making coffee and tea and slicing a seemingly infinite variety of cakes. While the adults worked, my cousins and I played games, watched TV, and gorged on sweets.

Yet amid all the merriment of these gatherings, with the food and fun and conversation, there was trouble. Arguments often broke out as the money was being counted. As I think back as an adult, I realize they were having trouble keeping the bills paid, despite the annual Christmas holiday rush, despite all the wonderful food. President Dwight Eisenhower's recession was putting people in unemployment lines in the late 1950s, and even our little bakery was feeling the stress.

The fights got even worse after my aunt and uncle and their kids went home, and my parents and I were left to clean up. My mother railed about my father's relatives, my dad tried to defend his brother and his family. The arguments often turned loud, generally building to my father slamming his fist on a table, my mother's eyes turning red and damp, and then, long stretches of silence between them.

As the recession got worse and the bakery business waned, those heady holiday seasons vanished into memory, and my parents soon told me they were closing the bakery for good. My father would get a job working in someone else's bakery, and we would move to a new neighborhood, leaving Germantown behind.

I didn't realize it, but because of the failure of their dream, my parents were about to come out of hiding as Jews in America.

Chapter 2

SKOKIE BLUES

THE MAN—SITTING BEHIND THE BATTERED METAL DESK wearing a wrinkled black yarmulke and rumpled brown suit, his tie hanging loosely over his ample paunch—did not inspire piety or awe. For as we students sat in our folding chairs awaiting our Hebrew lesson, he methodically went about cleaning his nose, seemingly oblivious to the many eyes riveted upon him.

I didn't yet know it, in the fall of 1962, but the interior of his nose was something of an obsession for the rabbi. Throughout the sessions yet to come, he would pick aggressively at it, and some of the kids really believed that was why he was named Rabbi Pickinley.

But, as I soon would learn, Rabbi Pickinley could recite prayers at astonishing speeds, tell stories from the Old Testament as if he had witnessed the events himself (or at least had heard about them from someone who had), and sing the prehistoric chants with a ring of authenticity. He must have known just about everything there was to know about being a Jew—he looked as if he had been one for ages.

On my first day in Hebrew school, in our new neighborhood, when the rabbi finally removed his well-worn hanky from his face and pushed it into his pants pocket to begin the class, he announced that he was not going to give us any instruction at all—at least not that day. Instead, he was going to turn the floor over to the students.

"Each of you should stand up, say your name, say something about yourself and your family, and say why you came to my Hebrew school," Rabbi Pickinley said.

Considering the appearance of the place—a jury-rigged, cramped, musty synagogue on the first floor of a converted Chicago bungalow—it seemed obvious even to an eight-year-old like me why everyone's parents had picked Temple Beth-El: because it happened to be in the neighborhood.

We didn't even have a classroom. Rabbi Pickinley had simply crowded a few chairs into what would have been the front room of the bungalow, the rest of the space devoted to the sanctuary, the ark, and the Torah. Nor were there classes for specific levels of Hebrew knowledge—kids my age to those on the verge of being bar mitzvahed were all thrown in together.

Looking at the tall, older students in the class made me nervous enough, and the prospect of standing up to talk about my family's interest in Judaism was terrifying. My father had only recently given me one tense little talk about our family's Jewish roots, specifically, I now guessed, in preparation for my enrollment in Rabbi Pickinley's school.

Shortly after we had moved into our new apartment in East Rogers Park, a working-class neighborhood on Chicago's North Side, my father had blurted out a few specifics about his years in the war.

"I was in a concentration camp, we had very little clothes, we just had some soup to eat, maybe once a day," he told me.

"What's a concentration camp?" I asked.

"A place where they kept Jews," my father said. "You know, we were prisoners. We worked.

"Sometimes they gave us toast, and I always tried to get the most burnt piece—it helped with diarrhea."

My mother chimed in when my father looked her way, but she revealed even less. "I was running, running, I didn't know where I was running," she said.

People were trying to kill her, she added, because they were killing Jews in her town, "my little Dubno," she called it.

That was about all I knew.

"My name is Howard Reich, and I have a mother and a father but no sisters or brothers, but I wish I did," I said.

"Hey, he's got two parents but no sisters or brothers—he's the Third Reich!" said one smart aleck, inspiring roars of laughter from the older kids. I didn't get the joke.

"Well," I continued before the surprisingly hostile crowd, which from here on would call me Third Reich, "we just moved here, we used to have a bakery on Lincoln Avenue, but now we live here.

"My father was in a concentration camp because he was Jewish," I said—the only thing I could think of saying that had anything to do with Judaism.

But as soon as I uttered that phrase—"concentration camp"—the kids burst out laughing again. Laughing! I couldn't believe it. Though I didn't understand what a concentration camp was, I knew I was being ridiculed, or my dad was.

"His father was in a concentration camp—did they move everyone around like cows?" one kid joked, to loud guffaws.

"Was it like summer camp, only worse?" said another.

Rabbi Pickinley did nothing more than ask the class to shush up while I was speaking. There was no righteous anger, no thundering lecture.

Maybe Rabbi Pickinley, like most others in the world in the 1950s and '60s, simply didn't want to hear again about a subject that was too dreadful to contemplate and impossible to explain, too overwhelming to come to terms with; or maybe he believed that kids are kids, that there was no way to get them to understand something that even adults couldn't make sense of.

Standing there, the object of so much laughter and derision, even my surname now a punch line, I silently promised myself that I would never again tell anyone about my father's concentration camp or my mother's years of running—what little I knew about it. And I kept that promise for decades to come. I would keep so quiet as to nearly forget the few words that they had told me.

I couldn't wait to see my uncle and aunt's new house in Skokie, wherever that was. My parents said it wouldn't be too far to drive from our apartment, maybe half an hour, and if my parents liked the neighborhood, maybe they would buy a house there, too.

So I climbed into the backseat of our Chrysler and watched the tall and gritty brick apartment buildings of the city's Far North Side give way to sleek, low-slung ranch homes. To me, it was like traveling to a place where movie stars might have lived, the grime and trash of the city yielding to spotless wide streets and thick blue-green lawns and a quiet that I had never encountered outdoors before.

When we finally pulled up in front of my relatives' house, I tore out of the car and ran inside the redbrick house, which was so new you still could smell the pine of the doorjambs and moldings. The walls of the kitchen, where visitors first entered, were covered with gleaming ceramic tiles that had been scrubbed spotless. As for the floors, they were like none I had ever encountered: even from the kitchen, I could see the white wall-to-wall carpeting that rolled uninterrupted from one room to another and looked soft enough to sleep on.

"Take off your shoes—don't take another step, you hoodlum," my aunt said to welcome me into her new house.

"You never walk with shoes in this house," scolded another aunt, who also was visiting.

"Only socks," my uncle added.

So I pulled off my shoes and started running around the place with my cousins, my parents entering the house a few beats after me. In a moment, they too had been ordered to lose the shoes, so they tiptoed into the living room in their stocking feet, where we all stared at the same strange sight: bright blue and gold furniture fitted top to bottom with taut, custom-made plastic coverings. The plastic presumably had been ordered to protect the sofa and chairs, but my aunts and uncle had gone one step further, placing layers of towels on top to protect the plastic.

"Be careful when you sit down," one of my aunts said to me. "The furniture is very expensive."

My cousins and I decided it would be safer to sit on the carpeted floor, where we played cards and board games and laughed loudly, while the grown-ups sat on the protected, perfect furniture and argued.

I couldn't wait to leave this place and go home.

Though Skokie was the height of luxury, our new Chicago neighborhood, in Rogers Park, was a lot more exciting.

Every morning, my mother took me by the hand and walked me to school, the two of us passing the fruit markets, laundromats, tailors, and coffee shops of Howard Street, a strip almost as colorful as Lincoln Avenue, though less Germanic. Poles, Hispanics, Jews, southern whites, the occasional black—everyone seemed to have packed into this corner of the world, on the North Side of Chicago near the lake. After mother deposited me at the school gates, she walked home again, only to pick me up a few hours later to take me home for lunch, then walk me back to school for the afternoon session, then meet me back at the school gates again at the end of the day.

Per our inviolable household rule, I was never allowed to walk the streets unescorted by my mother or another adult. Still, I always looked forward to seeing her waiting for me at the front of the school, ready to hear my news about the great or disastrous things that happened in class that day.

On some lucky days, my mother didn't take me home for lunch but instead walked me to a noisy diner where the waitresses screamed the orders to the cooks and the food flew out of the kitchen moments later. My mother and I ate with great pleasure our hamburgers smothered in grilled onions, and for dessert we always shared a pecan roll, lightly toasted. As we sat in a little booth built for two, my legs swinging under the table, I told my mom the names of my new friends in school, and she told me about the stores she had visited to get the best buys—where laundry was the cheapest, where apples were a few pennies less, where milk by the half-gallon was a steal. This was the high point of my day.

When we left the restaurant, my mother walked me across Howard Street in the direction of the school, making conversation with the crossing guard, the other parents, and sometimes, my friends. Often, she gave me a quarter to spend at the school store for games and knickknacks.

A few minutes after we returned home from school every day, my father arrived from work carrying bags of sweet rolls and fresh breads. After hugging him, I dove into these treats, as my father told my mother how well the breads had turned out that day. He often held up a Kaiser roll or a challah, informing my mother that the other bakers had asked for the details of his recipe, which he never would divulge.

Then my father took a nap for an hour or two, before waking up to make dinner, with my mother's help, in our tiny kitchen. While they cooked, the sound of an accordion often wafted up to our second-floor apartment from the dirt courtyard of our large building.

When my father heard this music, he always dropped everything and hustled outside to the back porch, listening raptly and usually whistling along. As soon as the song ended, my dad reached into his pocket, pulled out a coin or two, wrapped them in a piece of paper from his other pocket, and tossed the tiny package to the street musician, who tipped his cap in my father's direction.

Then after dinner my father went to bed, while my mother and I sat up late in the kitchen, she sipping black coffee and reading a magazine, I drinking hot tea and writing poems and stories. I penned tales of journeys on ships to distant places, of imagined adventures and heroics—often starring myself. When I showed these writings to my mother, she showered me with praise, encouraging me to write more. As we sat there, the world outside finally having nodded off to sleep, I tried desperately to stay awake as long as my mother did.

But that was never possible. My mother read and drank coffee all through the night in that kitchen, apparently never needing—or wanting—to go to bed.

There was a gentle knock on the front door of our apartment.

"Who is it?" my father asked.

"I'm from Encyclopaedia Britannica." That was all my dad needed to hear. He swung open the door and we saw a tall, slender black man wearing a somewhat dusty navy blue suit and a smile and carrying a bulging brown briefcase. My father stuck out his hand to the fellow, my mother observing warily from a distance. Quickly, the man was in our living room, his briefcase wide open, his wares spread out on our coffee table.

I also sat at the room's periphery, watching the salesman pitch to my dad in his usual after-work outfit: a pair of casual slacks, loose-fitting brown slippers, and a thin white undershirt revealing biceps so large that they were out of proportion for someone of his height.

"Mister Reich, someday your son is going to want to go to college," the salesman said, glancing toward my direction. "And he's going to have to be ready when he gets there. Encyclopaedia Britannica will make him ready."

My dad nodded enthusiastically, so the salesman pressed on.

"Anything your son wants to know—anything he needs to learn for school—is in these twenty-three volumes, plus the index," said the salesman. "These books will change your son's life," he added, offering a warm smile in my direction.

My dad quickly took the bait, talking about how he never had the chance to get much schooling, that his education was in a concentration camp.

When my dad said those words, I froze, figuring the salesman would burst out laughing, just as the kids in Hebrew school had done, but, no, the salesman nodded and seemed prepared to listen.

"Get me some cognac and make some coffee," my dad said to my mother, who headed directly to the kitchen and set to work.

Then my father told the salesman what had happened to him during the war—the fullest discourse on the subject I had ever heard.

"My father had a bakery in Poland, and all the boys in the family learned to work there," he said.

"When the Nazis came, they wanted to take my father away, but we begged them to take us kids, instead. I offered to go myself, and they took me.

"I worked in labor camps. We had to carry heavy metal rods on our backs. We had to walk on beams, high up on roofs, and if you fell, that's it, you're dead. But I never slipped once. I walked on those beams like it was nothing," my dad continued, clearly proud that he had been strong and athletic enough not only to survive but to excel under these terrible conditions.

"Later they took us to a concentration camp. I almost was dead, from typhus.

"Before they liberated us, we saw planes dropping bombs in the sky, and we knew the Americans were coming.

"That's when I knew I was going to live through it."

I was overwhelmed. Yet from this short description, not fifteen minutes long, I immediately sensed that my father was sparing the salesman and me the worst details, the full thrust of what had happened to him—a seventeen-year-old when the Germans invaded Poland in 1939.

"What happened, exactly, to my family I don't know," continued my father, adding that only a few survived. "The rest—killed."

The salesman listened, then offered stories he had heard about slavery and lynching in the South, my dad shaking his head at such barbarism.

What an unlikely pair these two men made: a Jewish baker from Poland who had lost most of his family, all of his youth, and any hope of emerging a musician or a painter, and a young black man from Chicago—or perhaps from somewhere in the South—selling encyclopedias door to door on a hot summer's day.

In the middle of the conversation, my mother brought drinks and cakes and sweet rolls, then sat at a far end of our green knit sofa listening quietly.

Eventually, the salesman returned to business.

"Now for about $500, these Encyclopaedia Britannicas will be yours—the price varies a bit depending on which kind of binding you would like."

He placed before my father three different book coverings: basic brown (cheapest of the three and unimpressive), ivory with a brown stripe near the top and bottom of each spine (mid-priced but very chic), and another that I can't remember but with a cost that was off the charts.

My dad picked exactly the one I wanted—ivory with the brown stripes—the salesman then going for broke by offering my father the chance to buy a decade's worth of the *Book of the Year*, which would arrive annually at our house.

"Once each *Book of the Year* arrives," the salesman assured my dad, "it will keep the rest of the encyclopedia up to date. It updates everything in the rest of the Encyclopaedia Britannica," he added, though I couldn't help wondering how one volume possibly could update the other twenty-three.

Finally, my dad wrote the check, then led the salesman to the front door.

"The encyclopedias will be here in a few weeks—call me if there are any problems," the salesman said on his way out. And the countdown began.

I helped my mother clear a special spot on the built-in bookshelf near the fireplace, estimating how much room we would need for the twenty-three volumes, all acquired for me.

About a month later, after school one day, the boxes were there in the living room, and I watched my dad open them up and place the books carefully, lovingly on the shelf. They were more beautiful and elegant and imposing than I had imagined. Each front cover carried the golden logo of Encyclopaedia Britannica, set above the number 1768, showing that the firm had been publishing for centuries. When all the books were positioned on the shelf—from volume 1, "A to Antarah," to volume 23, "Vase to Zygote," plus the *Index and Atlas*—a large part of all the knowledge of Western civilization stood right there, in our little living room, next to the TV set where we always watched the *Fight of the Week*.

I couldn't wait to plunge in, to find out what an "antarah" was, and a "zygote," and everything in between.

But as I reached for a volume, my mother and father shrieked together.

"Stop," my father said. "Don't touch those. Keep your greasy hands off of those books!"

"But I thought those books were for me," I said. "I thought you bought them for me. I thought the salesman said they were for your son, who needed them to go to college."

"Are you in college yet?" my father responded.

"You're too young for those books, you'll just make them dirty," said my mother. "You'll ruin them with your dirty hands. Wait till you get older."

"They're too expensive," my mother said. "Do you realize how hard your father had to work for those books?"

Every day my mother dusted those books, along with the rest of the house, and she said I could dust them, too. But they were never to be opened. Of course, on the occasions when my parents briefly stepped out of the house, I quickly pulled a volume from the shelf, found it impenetrable, and hurriedly returned it.

For years I had begged my parents for a sister or a brother—preferably a sister—and finally they complied.

The news that I finally wasn't going to be alone anymore, that I was going to have a sister, was almost as sweet as the arrival of the baby girl, Barbara Frances Reich. In early 1963, my parents told me that they named my new sister Barbara for Becia, my mother's mother, who was killed during the war; and Frances, for Franya, my father's sister, one of several siblings killed during the war.

I was beginning to realize that everything in our lives—from naming a baby to working in a bakery to sending me to Hebrew school—had something, although often something unspoken, to do with the war.

When my parents took me to the pediatrician for a checkup, she asked, with considerable excitement, if I understood what it meant to be born on April 19.

"Not really," I said.

"That's the date of the uprising of the Warsaw ghetto," the doctor informed me.

"Huh?"

"When the Jews fought back the Nazis in Warsaw.

"You're lucky you weren't born a day later," she added. "That's Hitler's birthday."

This subject kept turning up, though typically in strange, cryptic, incomprehensible ways. Never more significantly, though, than when my parents decided to move to Skokie, shortly after my sister's birth, for in the early 1960s Skokie was already well on its way toward becoming a nexus of Holocaust survivors.

Not that there were more survivors in Skokie than in Jerusalem or Brooklyn or Sydney, Australia—but there was a high percentage of survivors packed into a smaller amount of space. Roughly 8,000 survivors flocked to the tiny suburb, already more than 50 percent Jewish and barely ten miles square.

It was no coincidence that so many survivors found their way to this speck on the map. Jews had been unwelcome in most of Chicago's suburbs during the first half of the twentieth century, and by the 1950s they were eager to break out of their cramped enclaves on the city's South Side, the West Side, and eventually the North Side. Real estate developers saw a ready market in Jews who wanted to move up, and began advertising in Chicago's old Jewish neighborhoods that the gates to suburbia finally were swinging open—in Skokie. The lots may have been narrow and the houses compact, but Jews of all kinds—from World War II veterans to Holocaust survivors to wholly assimilated Americans whose families had lived in Chicago for generations—rushed in.

By 1958, no less than the Hebrew Theological College—a center of Jewish life in Chicago—moved from its longtime base on the city's West Side to a sprawling, sixteen-acre spread in Skokie, as sure a sign as any that Skokie had be-come safe territory for Chicago Jews, a shtetl in America, a ghetto in suburbia.

Survivors continued to snap up tiny homes in Skokie and to open synagogues, Hebrew schools, Jewish delis, kosher butcheries, Israeli bakeries, Old Country tailor shops, all the scenery and services of the Jewish world. On the High Holy Days, the public schools were practically empty.

Our new house, a squat two-bedroom ranch with one narrow bathroom, was the first place I ever saw my father post a mezuzah on the front door. A tiny sliver of scripture packed into a golden casing, the mezuzah told everyone who approached this doorway—everyone who could under-stand the symbol—that Jews lived inside. This was my fa-ther's first announcement since he came to America that he was a Jew.

That mezuzah, tilted at precisely the west-to-east angle that Jewish custom prescribes, changed everything. Now, during Hanukkah we lit the menorah, on Rosh Hashanah we went to the storefront synagogue down the street, on Yom Kippur we fasted while our stomachs growled and our throats burned. Suddenly, we were Jews. Even more remark-able, so was almost everyone else.

When we went to the butcher, Yiddish and Hebrew and Polish crackled in the air. When we went to temple, my fa-ther recited prayers almost as fluently as Rabbi Pickinley had, a stunning revelation.

"I learned in cheder—I loved cheder," my father said, re-ferring to an Orthodox Jewish education I had not known he had.

"In the Old Country, I sang the prayers in shul with such a falsetto voice, people looked around to see who was singing."

"But wait," I said. "If you know the Hebrew prayers so well, why do you only go to synagogue on Yom Kippur and Rosh Hashanah? Aren't we supposed to go every Shabbos? That's what they said in Hebrew school."

It seemed to me that I had caught my dad shirking.

"I don't have to go on Shabbos," my dad shot back. "After what I went through in concentration camp, I only have to go on the High Holidays."

"What does that have to do with going to shul?" I asked.

He gave me an angry stare.

My mother's behavior in synagogue was the antithesis of my dad's as he flew through the prayers. She was mute, rarely even opening the prayer book. As the service unfolded, she looked around the synagogue, studying its sea of faces. Later, she told me she didn't understand a word of what was happening in temple.

"I learned the Catholic prayers, when I was hiding with Catholics," my mother said to me, an extraordinary coincidence, I thought, since I had learned the Catholic prayers, too! What were the odds?

Yet now my mother and I found ourselves in a town—home, I suppose, although a strange one—where we saw Orthodox Jews wearing black suits and white shirts, with long curly hair hanging over their ears, parading to synagogue every Friday night and Saturday morning.

More remarkable still, most of the Jews of Skokie looked and sounded and acted just like my parents. They spoke with thick guttural accents, rolled their r's, and used sing-song phrasings; they yelled about politics in the Middle East; they even drew a horizontal line through the middle of the number seven when addressing envelopes or writing checks, just as they had been taught to do in school in Europe before the war.

Many of them had another odd feature in common—a long, blue-green number tattooed on the inside of their fore-arm. At a deli or at synagogue, I would see dozens of these numbers, some blurred a bit by the passage of time but un-mistakable nevertheless.

"They got those in concentration camp," my father said to me after I inquired.

"But why don't you have a tattoo?" I asked.

"Such a stupid question," he said.

Not yet willing to give up on the subject, I asked an un-cle why he didn't have a tattoo, either.

"Who knows? They didn't give them out when I was in camp," he said.

"How could you stand being there?" I asked him.

"For awhile, I doubted there was even a God," my uncle answered. "I looked up in the sky, and I thought, 'If there's a God, how could He let this happen?'"

That was the end of the conversation.

There may have been a house in Skokie that was smaller than ours, but I never encountered it. Our front hall gave anyone three steps—at most—before they were in the com-pressed living-dining area, which bordered the kitchen on one side and two slender bedrooms and the world's smallest bathroom on the other. But for the wall separating the living-dining room L-shape from the kitchen, you could travel the diameter of our house in about fifteen paces.

My father said he wanted something a little bigger— maybe with one-and-a-half bathrooms, but my mother had said no: she would buy only a house that they could pay for completely, in cash. No mortgage, no monthly payments, nothing owed to anyone.

If I was taking a bath and one of my parents wanted to use the facilities, I had to get out of the tub—in mid-soak— wrap a towel around myself, step out of the room, dripping, and wait for my parents to use the bathroom and blast the place with air freshener, a mist of chemicals settling on the cooling water in the tub. I climbed back in as, on some occasions, my other parent demanded use of the bathroom and the ritual repeated itself.

At this rate, a bath could take more than an hour. Under no circumstances, however, was I allowed to turn on the shower, which seemed a quick and easy alternative. It would be decades until I understood what must have been behind my parents' fierce aversion to showers.

In the evening, our house often shook with battles typically waged on the telephone, my father arguing with one relative or another, loudly smashing down the receiver or jumping as it was slammed down on him from the other end. It was hard to tell what all the yelling was about, but it often seemed to involve invitations that should have been forthcoming, gifts that should have been made, thank you notes that should have been written, and a thousand other perceived slights. These people simply did not trust each other, or anyone else, and even when—on the rare occasions—all the family members were on civil and speaking terms, the rancor bubbled up sooner or later.

Any family get-together, at anyone's house, eventually devolved into conflict, which often included a round of Holocaust one-upmanship.

"I was in camp with Anne Frank—she was right next to me," bragged one of my aunts.

"I was saved by Oskar Schindler," retorted another.

"I saw my grandfather's head cut off," said a third, apparently hoping to make up in gruesomeness what she lacked in celebrity cachet.

These discussions provided a gateway to other areas of dispute, the brothers and sisters and in-laws shouting at each other over what one person had said or done five minutes or five years ago.

If they weren't yelling at each other, they were firing away at the news of the day.

A report that Egyptian President Gamal Abdel Nasser threatened to push the Israelis into the sea prompted multiple relatives to promise that "he'll burn in hell." A dispatch that the USSR had voted against Israel in the United Nations meant for sure that Soviet ambassador Andrey Gromyko would choke on his food or drown in his pool.

Arabs, Russians, Germans, fascists, communists, goosestepping militarists, weakling pacifists, leftie Democrats, right-wing Republicans, goys, schwartzes, Ku Klux Klansmen, racists—they all were anti-Semites who would harm

Jews in a flash if they had a chance, according to my extended family.

Although I marveled at the lusty energy my relatives poured into their battles with the world and with each other, I wanted just as hard to tune it out. While they ripped into enemies real and perceived, I attempted to watch TV or flip through the newspaper or call my friends on the phone. I would use any distraction available.

But when they turned their firepower on me, I found myself outnumbered and outgunned.

"You wouldn't last ten minutes in the Holocaust," one aunt or another would say to me.

"You should kiss the ground every day that you have a mother and a father—do you know what I would give to have my parents?" my father hissed when I misbehaved or mouthed off.

"He doesn't know how good he has it," my mother would offer in support. "When I was your age, I was sleeping in the snow. But he has a big mouth to his parents."

No matter what I did wrong, my parents responded with telegraphic references to their youth—without once sitting me down to tell me the story of what happened. Perhaps they wanted to spare me unspeakable details. Perhaps they couldn't bear to relive the full narrative, much less place its entire burden on a child. Whatever the reasons, the Holocaust became a kind of verbal bludgeon, used often—but for punishment, not enlightenment.

Ultimately, I couldn't bear to hear the word, or say it, or contemplate anything related to it—reactions that did not go unnoticed by my family.

Periodically, when the subject came up, I tried to defend myself by countering that my family members weren't the only ones who had had it bad—so had the slaves.

"You're comparing slaves to the Holocaust?" my aunt Julia cried, in disgust.

"We wished we had it so good as the schwartzes."

There were joyous moments, too: My father taking my mother and me to the baker's union New Year's Eve party, where he danced exuberantly with a long line of women who admired his grace and quick feet. (My mother finessed the occasional slow dance, but otherwise watched off on the sidelines.) Or my father driving to my aunts' and uncles' houses to help shovel their cars out of snow or teach their kids how to drive, because he seemed to savor the chance to assist people in peril. Or my mother delivering a kiss to my dad, in the kitchen, when they thought I wasn't looking.

On rare occasions, my parents even took me to the movies, though only to see "Jewish" films such as *Exodus* or *Fiddler on the Roof*. And although we never went anywhere on vacations, my parents uninterested in ever leaving home, I savored my dad's annual week or two off of work, when tensions in our house diminished a bit.

During the rest of the year, however, our home settled into a strange but reliable routine. At night, my father slept in one bedroom, I in another, my sister on the living-room sofa, and my mother watched the hours go by in the kitchen, sipping black coffee late into the night. Throughout the evening, she walked to the front and back doors, checking to make sure that the locks had been dead-bolted shut, the little chain protector fastened into place. Three, four, five, ten times in a row she would tug at the door latch and push at the chain.

Long after all of us had fallen asleep, my mother turned off the lamp in the kitchen, but only after she had switched on a night-light. My mom then moved into the living room, near my sister's sofa, seated herself on the floor at the picture window and peered through the narrow space between the frill of the window shade and the sill underneath. I saw her perched at her lookout whenever I woke up to go to the bathroom. Silently, she stared through her self-styled peephole, studying the empty street or the occasional car that drove by.

I did not consider any of this unusual—it was the normal course of events in our home and, I presumed, every other home, where surely mothers stayed up all night protecting everyone who slept and checked the locks over and over.

Many nights, my father got out of bed a few times to take a couple of shots from a bottle of whisky he kept in the dining-room cabinet, before returning to bed. I assumed that he was trying to get himself to sleep as quickly as possible, knowing that he had to wake up to go to work in a bakery in just a few hours, at 2 or 3 in the morning.

The only time he seemed a bit more relaxed about sleeping was on the weekends, when he got out of bed at a normal hour and usually reported his dreams of the night before.

"I was killing Nazis good," he would sometimes say.

"I had a machine gun and I was knocking them all down."

My mother would nod approvingly but said nothing about her dreams, if she had any, or if she slept at all.

If Skokie had a celebrity, it was Mr. Eddie, whose store sold overpriced suits to every bar mitzvah boy in town. On a typical Saturday afternoon, the shop was overrun with skinny kids like me trying on three-piece Pierre Cardins and double-breasted Brooks Brothers that in six months would be too small and, therefore, useless. A constant stream of boys circulated through the store, running inside the dressing rooms wearing blue jeans and T-shirts but coming out in fancy pants and matching jackets that would acquire irremovable food stains shortly after they made their debuts at lavishly catered bar mitzvahs.

Mr. Eddie presided, his outsized mustache, frizzy halo of silver hair on a bald scalp, and own dressed-to-impress outfits apparently representing his vision of what a first-rate seller of high fashion was supposed to look like.

I couldn't wait to acquire my own bar mitzvah suit, which would be my payoff for enduring five years of dismal and mechanical Hebrew school lessons in order to learn the haftorah in preparation for the big event. Since I was becoming a man, I presumed that I would get to pick out the suit with my dad—an all-man bonding trip—but my mother insisted on coming along over my objections. As my father pulled one suit or another off the rack and handed it to me, my mother watched quietly.

Each suit I tried on Mr. Eddie proclaimed "perfect, just perfect—should we hem it up?"

Finally, my parents picked one—a beautiful, shiny dark number—and I was a step closer to the big day.

But for weeks still, my parents struggled with the seating chart for my bar mitzvah party, trying to keep track of which relatives and friends were not speaking to each other and which could at least tolerate sitting at the same table. My father drew endless versions of the seating chart, the circles representing the tables and the Xs signifying the guests, his diagram suggesting some mad, ever-shifting Jews-only football game.

Then there was the issue of who would be seated at tables toward the front of the synagogue and who would be relegated to the back. Even more delicate, however, was the question of who would get an honored spot at the head table. My father applied Talmudic considerations to these plans, hoping he had made the right decisions, though he was well aware that there was no way he was going to make everyone happy.

The day before my bar mitzvah, my father was to repeat the ritual that his father had done with him, and all religious Jews have done with their sons through the ages: officially showing me how to wrap the *tfillin* on my forearm and my forehead. Having learned the basics in Hebrew school, I couldn't wait to do the steps with my dad, but on that great morning, he rushed through the process so fast—and mouthed the prayers so elliptically—that we must have finished in thirty seconds.

I was startled and disappointed. It was as if he wanted to get through it as fast as possible, without so much as looking at me. I did not understand his haste, though, in retrospect, perhaps it conjured up memories for him that were too searing to bear and too sacred to revisit.

Otherwise, my bar mitzvah service proceeded surprisingly smoothly, with no open warfare, though the party the next day proved to be a classic family event, some relatives fuming at where they had been seated. Others were furious that they hadn't been called to participate in the candle-lighting ceremony—a nonreligious, somewhat concocted rite in which a few close family members are invited to help the bar mitzvah boy light his cake, while the emcee recites a few gushing words about the relatives who were chosen.

For weeks afterward, my father endured phone calls from those who complained that they had been slighted, insulted, or worse, the conversations often ending in the usual way.

I had to find a way out of this. It would take several years until I did.

Chapter 3

SWING TIME

I KNEW NOTHING OF GENE KELLY OR LESLIE CARON WHEN I happened upon *An American in Paris*, the glorious film musical, one night on TV in the basement of our house. Even in black and white, on our fifteen-inch television screen, the sight of the two of them aswirl in the film nearly overwhelmed me, a riot of movement and rhythm and melody of a sort I had never imagined might exist.

As the muscular Kelly raised the lithe, slender Caron up above him, streaks of light flashed across the nighttime sky. Caught up in their reverie, the couple barely noticed the fountain spraying streams of water just inches away. Slowly, the lovers embraced, pulled apart, then came together again, light and half-light playing on their faces while music surged in the background—violins and horns and winds crying out all at once.

Even if the romantically charged duet that brings *An American in Paris* to a climax hadn't seduced me, the scenes preceding it very nearly did. I smiled at the whimsy of Kelly soft-shoeing atop a baby grand, while Oscar Levant played Gershwin's "Tra-La-La" on the keys; I laughed aloud while Kelly, Levant, and Georges Guetary cavorted in a French café in three-quarter time; I held my breath as Kelly and Caron slow-danced along the River Seine while "Our Love Is Here to Stay" whispered in the background; and I watched with awe and disbelief as Levant—plushly suited in white tie and tails—rapidly hammered the keys of a Steinway grand playing the finale of Gershwin's Concerto in F.

This was it. Here was the answer to the question still loosely formed in my mind: How do I escape the anger and the noise and the insults and the feuds that perpetually roiled my family? Rhythm, movement, jazz, swing, color (even in black and white!), light—art, I discovered, by accident, allowed me an escape, even though I still sat in the same old Naugahyde vinyl chair in the same tiled-floor basement of the same tiny home in Skokie.

The next afternoon, when my father came home from work—hot and tired but, as always, carrying waxed paper bags stuffed with fresh breads and sweet rolls—I told him I needed a piano, immediately. I needed to learn to play. I didn't say why, I didn't explain my two revelatory hours of the night before.

To my utter amazement, my father did not immediately dismiss the notion, nor did my mother. I had been ready to recite a litany of reasons they should spend hard-earned money on an expensive instrument, yet they didn't ask for one. Perhaps my dad—who once hoped I might play the accordion, like him—felt that a piano was close enough. Perhaps my mother, who always said that school was crucially important, though she had seen so little of it, considered the piano another form of learning. I never asked.

A few weeks later, it arrived at our house: a big, bright, sleek, state-of-the-art . . . electric organ! Not exactly what I had envisioned, but it was close enough, in that it at least had black-and-white keys. In fact, like most such instruments, it offered not one but two keyboards, plus a series of pedals for the bass notes.

I was mildly amused but still elated. With the arrival of that organ, I felt as if I were about to emerge from a long stupor, as if I had spent the past decade and a half or so in a thick fog, unaware of who or what I was, and now these black-and-white keys promised to explain it all.

I practiced from the moment I came home from high school to the moment I went to bed. Staking this claim on the living room left my father to head into the kitchen to talk—or shout—on the telephone while I struggled to master the kind of elementary pieces that five-year-olds across America could handle easily. With this kind of devotion, I quickly made up for lost time. Within a couple of months, I was playing J. S. Bach's Inventions, intricate keyboard pieces in which three distinct lines of melody and rhythm unfold.

My parents took some pride in my progress, even asking me to play the organ for my aunts and uncles when they visited one evening. Flattered, I positioned myself at the instrument and silently gathered my thoughts, the relatives seated quietly in the sofa and chairs nearby. My fingers next began to caress the keys, producing long and sinuous strands of melody—it sounded magnificent.

Or at least it did to me. But as the music progressed, I thought I heard soft tittering in the background. So as my fingers walked the keyboards, I tilted my head almost imperceptibly to one side, so that I could see what was happening behind my back: one of my uncles was performing a bit of pantomime, pressing his palms together, as if he were praying. Meanwhile, his eyes looked heavenward as he mumbled some kind of nonsense incantation—as if the music I played had transported him to church. I was hurt, slightly, but not surprised.

After a few months, I persuaded my parents that I needed a real piano—an organ simply wasn't the same, and they went along, purchasing a used Wurlitzer spinet, the smallest piano made. Designed to be pushed up against a wall, it fit like a glove in a corner of our cramped living room. When it arrived, I redoubled my efforts, rehearsing relentlessly.

When I wasn't at the piano, I was in the public library borrowing recordings, then wearing down the grooves of Bach's shattering Toccata and Fugue in D Minor, Beethoven's mysterious *Moonlight* Sonata, and Debussy's sensuous Etudes for Piano. I didn't understand how it was possible for the pianists on these recordings—Arthur Rubinstein, Vladimir Horowitz, Oscar Levant, Sviatoslav Richter—to coax such intoxicating sounds from eighty-eight keys, how they were able even to read scores that must have contained an ocean of notes.

One night, while aimlessly flipping through a forest of junk that had been jammed into a cabinet in our basement,

I came across something unexpected: piles and piles of LP recordings. Stunned, I pored over black vinyl discs of the Philadelphia Orchestra playing Debussy's *La Mer,* Enrico Caruso singing operatic arias, Arthur Rubinstein performing Chopin ballades, Tony Bennett singing hits of the big-band era—a mother lode of great music just sitting there, awaiting my discovery.

"Those are my records," my father said, when I asked about the stash. "When I came to Chicago, I went to Marshall Field's, and you could listen to the records there before you bought them," he said.

"Your father always was buying records," my mother added. "Every week he had new records in his hands."

My dad a record collector? Incredible.

"We went out dancing, too, to the Aragon Ballroom," in Uptown, my mother said. "We saw movies and shows at the Chicago Theatre. We ate at Fritzel's, downtown."

Amazing.

I quickly worked my way through my father's record collection, then went back to devouring the LPs at the library. From the Austro-Germanic Beethoven and Brahms I moved on to the Americans Gershwin and Copland, and from there to the jazz piano god Art Tatum and the stride keyboard genius James P. Johnson and the whispering poet of the alto saxophone Art Pepper—jazzmen who seemed to me every whit as great as Rubinstein and Horowitz but freer, bolder, and less tethered to something that someone else had written for them to play. The jazz musicians were making it up as they went along, composing as it happened, playing sequences of notes and rhythms no one had played before them and no one ever would play again.

I couldn't comprehend how an alto saxophonist could whisper as hauntingly as Pepper did playing Michel Legrand or how a piano could thunder as it did when Tatum riffed on "Tea for Two," arpeggios racing up and down the keyboard, scales flying at speeds that must have brought Horowitz himself to despair.

I had to see these musicians, I had to find out how they did it.

With some trepidation, my high school friend Phil and I conspired to explore the mysterious world of Chicago night-life. Having similarly immersed himself in the exotic sounds of jazz, Phil—a tall, skinny fellow whose face seemed perpetually buried in a book—insisted that the two of us, together, could finesse our way into a jazz joint, even if we were under age. So on a hot summer's night, we rode the el to Fullerton Avenue in the city and walked a few blocks east to the Jazz Showcase, a makeshift club up a steep flight of stairs above a bar on North Lincoln Avenue. The man at the door asked us how old we were, we nervously lied that we had turned eighteen, paid our money—no questions asked—ordered a couple of beers, and watched something like a hurricane spin the room.

This wasn't just jazz—it was Sun Ra, the fabled visionary who insisted he was more than 1,000 years old and had arrived from some distant spot in the Milky Way. "Space is the place," he cried, and he looked the part, wearing an Afro-centric headdress and billowing, glittering robes. As he paraded on stage, he presided over a screaming big band that fired off great plumes of energy, while fire-eaters, acrobats, dancers, gymnasts, and shamans coursed through the crowd.

Clearly we weren't in Skokie anymore. A couple of gaunt, bespectacled, acne-faced teenagers were beholding, for the first time, a free-form, multimedia eruption in swing time— jazz, Chicago style, with palpable hysteria and frenzy.

So this was what waited outside our little suburb. This was what you could do if you chose not to spend your evenings arguing and slamming down the phone.

Phil and I started visiting the jazz clubs regularly. We stared wide-eyed as tenor saxophonists Al Cohn and Zoot Sims brayed mercilessly at one another. We found ourselves pinned to our seats as Sonny Stitt blew immense bebop blasts from the bell of his horn. We reveled in the seamless, silken strands of melody that Teddy Edwards nonchalantly pulled from his saxophone.

Then we moved on to the strip joints. Though nervous that we might get mugged, we plunged ahead, handing over a steep fifteen-dollar cover charge at the Candy Store off Rush Street, paid the two-drink minimum, and watched in awe as women of various sizes and shapes danced mechanically to recordings of raunchy blues and cheesy R & B, revealing things that no high school girl ever revealed in our presence. After the show, the strippers came over to our table to get us to buy them overpriced drinks. We jumped at the chance. Never before had we sat so close to women wearing so little, saxophones crying and trumpets grinding on the sound system.

After these thrilling nights out, the return to Skokie seemed all the more grim, though some evenings were worse than others. On one evening, after spending a few hours reading at the library, I happened to run into Phil, and we began conversing in the parking lot after the place closed for the night at 9 P.M. For an hour, or so, we stood near our cars—or rather, our parents' cars—talking jazz, movies, TV, girls, whatnot.

By around 10 P.M., we parted, each taking the five-minute drive home. But as I approached my house and backed into a parking spot, I noticed a squad car behind me. Out of some kind of reflex that I cannot explain, I put my father's light blue Ford into forward gear and sped off, the cop immediately pursuing me. I, still inexplicably, drove right around the block, returned to the house and saw my parents on the front steps, waving frantically at me. The police car again parked right behind me.

With dread and confusion, I stepped out of the Ford and walked slowly toward the house, the cop a few paces behind me as I approached my parents.

"Where were you—do you know what time it is?" my mother screamed, as my father joined in, yelling the same.

"We had to call the police. Do you know the trouble you caused?" my dad said, as the cop began to fill out his report.

"Wait a minute," I argued. "I was just at the public library, I ran into Phil, and we were talking."

The cop handed the report to my father, who looked as if he were going to kill me, while my mother remained in panic mode. Then we all went into the house, and my father took a couple of shots from the bottle of whisky he kept in the dining-room cabinet, as the household slowly settled again into its usual nocturnal ritual.

By now, a year and a half after I had started piano lessons, I was playing Mozart sonatas and Bach preludes and fugues, my repertoire growing in size and complexity every month. At this rate, I concluded, with the optimism of youth, I would be Horowitz in, oh, about a year or two. And I continued to nurse a long-held ambition to be a writer, having penned stories and poems incessantly since childhood. Over the years, though, the fantasy tales of my youth had evolved into commentaries on politics and social issues, published in the high school newspaper and modeled on writers such as Mike Royko and Sidney J. Harris in the *Chicago Daily News*.

"Do you know how hard it is to get to be a writer?" my father asked, when I told him of my career choice during junior year at Niles East High School.

"You should be a lawyer or a doctor—or at least an accountant," added my mother.

A lawyer? An accountant? Did they have no idea of who I was?

Considering how many hours my parents spent reading the paper every day, my dad laughing aloud at Royko's wit in the *Daily News*, I was surprised by the seriousness of their opposition.

They needn't have worried, though, for by the time the acceptance letter arrived from Northwestern University's Medill School of Journalism, I had become so immersed in

music that newspapering didn't even seem to be in the picture anymore. Instead, I decided to request an audition at
the university's School of Music before the fall term began.
If I was lucky, I would never have to set foot inside a journalism classroom.

Figuring, sensibly enough, that my parents would be further appalled at my sharp left turn into music, I didn't say a
word about it. To avoid arousing suspicions on my audition
day, a sweltering August afternoon in 1972, I did not ask
my father to borrow his car. I simply stepped out of the
house, hopped onto my red-and-white Sears bike, and pedaled about an hour to Evanston, arriving soaked from
perspiration.

I locked up my bicycle, walked into the School of Music to
dry off, and heard scales and arpeggios and Brahms sonatas
and Chopin ballades echoing through the building—some of
the same pieces I had listened to on our record player at
home. I quickly started to doubt that a big-time music school
like this—crowded with such accomplished pianists—was
going to welcome me. Maybe they would throw me out as a
fraud before I even laid my hands on the keys.

When my damp shirt seemed about as dry as it was going
to get, I walked up a flight of stairs, found room 204, and
knocked on the door of Prof. Donald Isaak, who had agreed
to hear me.

"So what are we going to play today?" asked Dr. Isaak.

We're not going to play anything, I thought—I'm the one
sticking my neck out here.

I recited my repertoire, and he invited me to choose either
of the two grand pianos dominating his studio. I picked the

Steinway—as if I could play such a momentous performance on a Yamaha—and seated myself on the black leather bench. As I began performing Bach's Prelude and Fugue no. 2 in C Minor, from the *Well-Tempered Clavier*, Dr. Isaak's oscillating fan blasted a hot stream of air at my back every two and a half bars or so. Despite the distraction—will that fan never stop? or could it at least hit on the beat?—the Bach went off smoothly.

Confidence gathering in my sweaty fingertips, I moved on to music of Felix Mendelssohn, then concluded with a fiery Spanish dance by Granados, my right hand throwing off octaves at an aggressive tempo. The piano shook.

When I finished, I didn't know if I was supposed to bow or not, but in the absence of applause, I simply swiveled around on the bench cautiously, facing my interlocutor.

"How long did you say you've been studying the piano?" Dr. Isaak asked.

"About a year and a half," I answered, softly and with some shame, fearing that Dr. Isaak might consider my brief tenure at the piano an instant disqualification for admission to the music school.

"You do amazing work," he said.

Pardon me?

"You start in September."

I was in! I shook Dr. Isaak's huge hand, bolted down the winding staircase toward my bicycle, and pedaled for another hour to get home, the greatest ride of my life.

Now came the hard part—telling my parents. Since we were going out to dinner that night, I decided to deliver the good/bad news at the restaurant, Mister Ricky's, a Jewish deli where arriving guests first laid eyes on one hundred salamis hanging from the wall. Perhaps the social setting would soften the blow, I thought. Once the matzo ball soup arrived, I took a deep breath and forged ahead.

"Hey, guess what?" I said, as if I were about to announce something terrific but incidental, though I doubted it would be received either way.

"I've decided I'm not going to journalism school after all."

This prompted both my parents to put their spoons in their soup bowls and leave them there.

"I'm going to become a piano major!"

My dad didn't miss a beat.

"You'll never get in to music school."

And now came a moment I had long anticipated, knowing what I would say to prove to my parents that I had seized control of my life.

"I already did. This afternoon I auditioned, and they've accepted me. I'm starting in four weeks."

My parents were silent. So I repeated myself, to make sure they heard me.

I should have been able to predict the next turn in the conversation, but I didn't.

"Newspapers are much better," my father said.

"Look at Mike Royko," he added. "Everybody knows him."

"How are you going to make a living?" asked my mother. "Playing in taverns? You'll be a bum."

During the years I went to Northwestern, I never dared to bring home the various shiksas I dated. I remembered hearing about a cousin who dated a non-Jew; when her parents found out, she wished she hadn't. So the Christian beauties at Northwestern who welcomed me into their arms never met my parents or even heard about them.

By my senior year, having finally mastered and performed at Northwestern my beloved Concerto in F of Gershwin—the same piece that had launched my adventure in music that night in my parents' basement—I began to drift away from the idea of becoming a concert pianist. For starters, practicing the craft was unnerving me. During my required six to eight hours a day, I yearned to go out and explore the world outside my rehearsal room. Yet whenever I went to a movie or a party or even a restaurant, I kept saying to myself, "I should be practicing."

This conflict made me a nervous wreck, and, to drive myself battier, I often thought of what Oscar Levant had said about his own career: "I wanted to be Horowitz, but the job was taken."

Considering the transforming effect that *An American in Paris* had had on me, I started to realize that actually I wanted to be Oscar Levant—confidant of Gershwin, leading interpreter of his work, internationally known pianist, occasional movie star—but that job, too, was taken.

So I hit on the idea of writing about music, combining two passions. Before finishing my degree in piano performance, I began freelancing on music for the *Chicago Daily News*—Mike Royko's paper!—and instantly realized that I enjoyed criticizing, or praising, other people's playing more than actually performing myself.

At home, my parents' anguish over their past, stated or un-stated, intensified in one notorious incident that no one would have been able to predict. For in 1978, Frank Collin, a short man wearing a brown shirt and a swastika armband, be-gan appearing on TV, regaling swarms of reporters, promising that his neo-Nazi group had decided to stage a march—in Skokie.

To me, the guy seemed like a crackpot, a joke, a pathetic little man playing to the cameras and relishing the atten-tion. If Collin had announced that he would lead his neo-Nazi march in a suburb such as Naperville or Flossmoor or Arlington Heights, he wouldn't have gotten more than a moment on any station, if that.

But the prospect of Nazis parading in uniforms in Skokie—an otherwise ordinary suburb that happened to be overflowing with Holocaust survivors—made Collin and his little band of provocateurs big news.

We all watched on TV while Collin ranted and raved, and I saw my dad's face turn ashen. In a minute Dad was on the telephone, warning in Yiddish one relative or another about the return of the Nazis. He seemed to make no distinction between the real thing and this sorry facsimile. Why, I realize now, should I have expected him to? The swastika was the same, the message was identical, and hadn't Hitler himself been something of a laughingstock, a small, yammering man, existing on the margins before 1933, when he became chan-cellor of Germany and its emerging dictator?

For my father, perhaps, only the language and the date on the calendar had changed.

As the media circus gathered its audience that fall of 1978, my father was beside himself with rage and dread, pacing the living room, staring at the street from the open front door, lamenting the events to anyone who would listen.

My mother didn't say a word—at least none that I can remember. She exiled herself to the kitchen, working, scrubbing, forgetting herself—or trying to—in a never-ending circuit of duties.

"I'll get a bat and break his head if he marches," said my father, and he would have relished the opportunity. But he never got the chance.

After months of legal battles and relentless media coverage that agitated my parents and thousands of people like them, Collin prevailed in his court fight to obtain a permit to march, but he decided not to come to Skokie after all. Instead, he took his parade to Humboldt Park, in Chicago. Perhaps he heard that he might be greeted in Skokie by men and women who shared my father's point of view and that the local police might be inclined to look the other way.

Even when the fury died down, my father, at least, couldn't get over it.

"Too bad I didn't get to break Frank Collin's head," he often said.

Shortly after I was hired by the *Chicago Tribune* in 1983, I began dating a city-desk copy editor, Pam Becker. After a few months she began to wonder why I wasn't introducing her to my folks.

"What's the problem?" she asked, perhaps imagining that she had hooked up with a commitment-phobic man.

"How about if I start by just introducing you to my sister?" I said, trying to buy time.

Yet I knew that a meeting was inevitable. At thirty, an age when most sons have introduced their parents to a long line of love interests, I was about to bring a girlfriend home for the first time.

"My parents are a little different from most parents," I told Pam, trying to prepare her—and myself—for the big meeting.

"They're Holocaust survivors, they speak with thick accents, they consider everyone suspicious, and the only thing you've got going for you is that you're Jewish," I said, realizing right then that Pam may have been the first Jewish woman I ever dated.

"So let's meet them already," answered Pam.

Maybe she knew something I didn't, for from the moment Pam walked into my parents' Skokie home, my dad seemed smitten. Within minutes, he was asking my mother to bring beverages and sweet rolls from the kitchen, taking out his accordion to show Pam how well he played, displaying the oil paintings and pencil drawings he had made immediately after the war.

My mother said very little, but she didn't object, either.

"I think they liked me," Pam said later, with typical understatement. But who could resist this woman, with her sharp intellect, warm personality, and gentle manner? I further concluded that because I never had brought anyone home before, my parents probably expected the worst—whatever that might be—and were pleasantly surprised.

When Pam and I announced our engagement and informed my parents that Pam wouldn't be changing her last name, however, they went haywire.

"What's the matter with you—she won't even take your name?" my father demanded, though I insisted that I loved the idea of marrying a woman with an identity of her own.

"But what will it say on the doorbell of your apartment?" my mother wondered. We'll manage, I assured her.

So the prewedding rituals began, Pam and I busily lunching and dining with relatives and friends, to tell them the news and receive their unsolicited advice.

One such dinner proved disastrous for me.

As a relative of Pam's picked at her salad, she began describing in horrific detail a new movie she had just seen: Shoah, a nine-hour epic on the Holocaust. Though she knew of my parents' background, she lustily offered a blow-by-blow account.

To hear someone speaking to me so cavalierly—over a shrimp salad—about the Holocaust, a word I still could not bring myself to say, in a blithe recapping of what she considered the most entertaining movie release of the week was more than I could bear.

"The people in the film said they could smell the bodies burning," said the relative, "and they saw the smoke rising up in the sky from the ashes of those people!

"In the film, they discussed the ovens where they put people and the concentration camps, where the inmates looked like skeletons."

Did this woman have any idea that this was my family she was talking about, not mere shadows flickering on a movie screen? I gnashed my teeth, too stunned to ask the relative to stop.

When Pam and I got back to her apartment, I sat down on the bed and began weeping uncontrollably—the first time I ever cried over the Holocaust.

Shortly after Pam and I were married, my father asked me if I wanted to go to Poland with him and my mother, plus an aunt and uncle and various cousins and distant relatives and friends—the typical cavalcade of Reichs and in-laws and others—to see where the family lived before the war. The thought of spending two weeks in Poland with all of those people kept me in the United States.

For weeks, my parents prepared for the trip, packing enough clothes to spend half a year there, it seemed to me.

"Do you want us to bring you anything from Poland?" my father asked me, and it took a few minutes before I could think of something.

"Anything having to do with Chopin would be great," I said, showing in that phrase, I now realize, that I utterly missed the import of this trip, my parents' first visit to their barely discussed past. After all the decades of rage from my father and his relatives—and near silence from my mother— they finally were returning to the scene of the crimes.

And I was asking for a souvenir of Chopin.

A couple of weeks later, when my parents returned, my dad talked about finding the home in Sosnowiecz where he had spent his youth and from which he had been taken away by the Nazis. He marveled at how frightened the Poles who now lived there became when he appeared with his entourage, the locals believing that the old Jews had come back to reclaim their stolen homes.

"We had to talk hard to convince them we didn't want the house back—it was a *shanda*"—a disgrace—"how it looked today, filthy, terrible," my father said.

"How about mom's home, in Dubno?"

"We didn't go," said my mother. "Why do I want to go there?"

"I thought that was the point of this trip," I said.

"No—we went to see where your father lived. He wanted to show it to me."

As we stood around the freshly dug grave, tears rolled down everyone's face, but no one seemed more pained than my father. This was peculiar, because the funeral was for some-one he had met just once, at my wedding—my wife's grand-mother.

Yet my father's complexion had turned pale, and if I read his movements correctly, he appeared to be clutching his stomach under his large coat. He left the graveside before the funeral ended, my mother later explaining that he had been suffering excruciating stomach pains for months.

Though my father hated visiting doctors, he finally went to see one.

"Your father is very sick—he needs an operation," my mother said on the phone a couple of days later, and Pam and I immediately drove to their house to try to understand what was happening.

"I have a little tumor, so I have a little operation," my fa-ther said. In fact, he had a large tumor and was going to have his stomach removed, I would learn from the surgeon a few days later.

On the way home, a few blocks from my parents' Skokie house, I pulled the car over to the curb and wept.

I couldn't believe it. No one could believe it. No one who knew my father could understand how a man who looked as if he could lift a house, who had never missed a day's work and had retired from the bakery just a year earlier, could possibly be so ill.

My sister, Barb, who was married and living in California, returned to Chicago to help our parents through the ordeal. After the surgery, a scattering of relatives came to the hospital room to visit my ailing dad, but, of course, the feuds raged on. Most of the uncles and aunts and cousins never appeared. And some who did, perversely refused to speak to my mother, ignoring her while conversing for hours with her husband. But my mother was unfazed, planting herself at my father's hospital bed and refusing to move, regardless of how many relatives pretended she wasn't there.

When my father returned home, my mother's chronic insomnia finally paid off, for he was required to take certain medications at particular intervals during the course of the night. There was no need to set an alarm clock, for my mother was always there, with pill and glass of water at hand.

The doctors were surprised, though I wasn't, at my father's swift recovery. Within months of his radiation and chemotherapy regimen, his thick, silver-red hair grew back, his strength rebounded, his hands—those immense, slightly orange palms—looked as if they belonged to a man who hadn't been sick a day.

"I can feel my strength again," my father said, clenching his enormous fists, like some biblical figure who has been given one last and fleeting moment of his former power and glory.

"I could pick up a car," he said, and I believed him. Not long after his recovery, in fact, he bragged about how he had tested his strength—and his nerve—at a traffic light. A couple of teenage hooligans in another car had given him the finger, but then, to their misfortune, they found themselves positioned at a stop light alongside him.

My father pulled out the rusted tire iron that he always stored under the driver's seat, opened the door of his car, and headed toward theirs. Before he reached them they sped through the red light, fearing for their lives.

"I bet you their pants were full," my father said, proudly.

He was back, I thought, back to his magnificent athletic form, back to the combination of defiance and anger that had enabled him to survive. But then his stomach pains began again, and he returned to the hospital for the last time.

On a Saturday afternoon, as the nurses prepared to move him from intensive care to a regular room, my mother became frantic, positioning herself in front of the bed, refusing to allow anyone to move him. We spent more than an hour persuading her that no one was giving up on Dad—just that the most that anyone could do right now was to make him comfortable.

My mother finally relented, accompanying my father to his new room, where morphine intended to dull his pain left him dazed and confused. At some moments, he rose up from his hospital bed, saying, "I have to go, I have to get out."

My sister, her husband, and I all had to push him back into the bed, his strength still greater than that of any two of us.

For days on end, my mother rarely left his bedside, sleeping fitfully on the sofa outside his room, washing up in his bathroom. He was not visited by the aunts and uncles whose snowy sidewalks he had shoveled, the cousins he had taught to drive or chauffeured from one event to another.

Then, in the middle of the night, my phone rang at home, and I heard my mother's voice.

"Your father isn't moving," she said.

"Is he breathing?" I asked.

"I don't know. I don't think so," my mother said.

I threw on some clothes, raced to the hospital, and by the time I got there, my father indeed had been pronounced dead. It was early in the morning of February 16, 1991.

My mother looked utterly lost.

The morning of my dad's burial, my sister, her husband, Pam, and I convened before the funeral at the Skokie house, my mother crying and talking softly but constantly.

I don't remember everything she said, but one sentence I could not forget: "I may as well crawl into the coffin with him," she whispered.

About a hundred people came to the service at Weinstein's Funeral Home near Skokie—old men and women with numbers on their forearms, bakers who had worked with my father in shops across the city, bosses, doctors, friends.

Many of my aunts and uncles and cousins did not attend. A former boss of my dad's wrote a speech that someone read aloud, the text zeroing in on my parents' trip to the Old Country a few years earlier.

"The family had gone back to Poland and to the town of Robert's birth and early life," the speaker said. "Remember that the occupation of the Nazis had indelibly changed all the memories of joy into macabre scenes of deprivation, torture, and unspeakable horror.

"As the family walked through the town, they came upon the old family home, now lived in by some elderly lady, and when they came up to the house, the lady ran out and started to run away—probably to hide.

"It was Robert who went after her and called out to her not to run, for he understood the circumstances of her living there, and he was not going to make trouble but only wanted to look again at his childhood home . . . such kindness in the ashes of such hell."

At the grave, the rabbi said a few words about a man he hardly knew. No one could concentrate on what he was saying anyway.

We walked through the winter mud back to the cars, then returned to the house in Skokie, where we sat shivah for three days.

I couldn't remember the prayers I had been taught in Hebrew school, so my sister's husband led the services in the house, while I silently moved my lips, mimicking prayer.

Eventually, everyone went home, and my mother remained in the house. For the first time since 1952, when she met my father, she was alone. Together, it seems, my mother and father had managed to stave away the demons of their past. By working ferociously hard at the bakery, by pouring every cent he earned into the well-being of his family, by sending his kids to college and reaching a richly deserved—if tragically short-lived—retirement, my father had triumphed over a horrific youth. Though nightmares disturbed his sleep and deep-seated anger often flashed into the open, he pressed relentlessly forward in life. Perhaps nothing soothed the wounds of his past more than his decision to marry my mother, a damaged woman with frostbitten hands and feet whom he rescued and made whole.

Now my dad, the one person in whom my mother had placed all of her trust, was gone.

And no one—not my mother or my sister or me—understood the implications.

Chapter 4

The Past Returns

A FEW WEEKS AFTER MY FATHER'S DEATH, I JABBED AT THE doorbell of my mother's Skokie home a few times, but there was no response. I hit the bell again and again, then started to panic—why wasn't she answering?

So I scampered down the front steps, squeezed behind the bushes in front of the house, and pressed my nose against the glass, hoping I wouldn't get picked up as a Peeping Tom. Though the shade was drawn, I could see a trace of light just below it and peered inside. As I did, I realized that I was looking through the same pane of glass my mother had spent much of my childhood sitting behind, as she perched on the living-room floor night after night, scanning the quiet streets of Skokie for signs of danger.

Squinting, I saw Mom, a tiny gray-haired woman in a black skirt, beige blouse, tan stockings, white sneakers, and tightly drawn apron aggressively vacuuming the shag carpeting underfoot. The roar of the Electrolux had prevented my mother from hearing the doorbell. She pushed and pulled the machine, covering a single patch of carpet over and over—like a farmer tilling the same piece of soil—until she moved on to the next strip and repeated the process.

After I rapped my knuckles on the window a few times, my mother approached the shade, pulled it up a few inches, and noticed me with a start, abruptly waving me to the front door, which she finally swung open.

"What are you doing in the bushes? Are you crazy?" she asked.

"Trying to get your attention!" I shouted. "I've been ringing the doorbell for five minutes."

"I didn't hear a thing—you should ring harder," said my mother.

A few minutes later, my wife, Pam, met me at the house, as we had planned, and we asked my mother if she still wanted to go out to dinner with us. My mother said she would if we agreed to dine at a Jewish deli, suggesting either The Bagel or Barnum and Bagel—basically any restaurant with the word "bagel" in it.

Over matzo ball soup my mother talked about her shopping outings, her phone conversations with my sister, Barb, in California, and a recent visit to the cemetery where my father was buried. Because my mother didn't know how to drive, she had to take two buses to get to Shalom Memorial Park, in Arlington Heights, and two more to get back, but it turned out that that was the least of her problems.

"I tried to cry at your father's grave, but I couldn't," my mother said.

"I don't know why. I couldn't cry until I was home."

Then she added, "Your father still talks to me. I see his face on the wall, very clear. Sometimes he follows me to different rooms, and he gives me advice on what to do, how to do things the right way."

I made little of this comment, presuming that most new widows talked to the ghosts of the men they had lost.

On other occasions, however, my mother acted in ways that utterly baffled me. Usually, when Pam and I came to visit, my mother was in the midst of doing laundry—"at least three loads a day," she bragged—and we were mystified as to how one woman possibly could generate so much wash. We were perplexed, too, by her daily trips to the grocery store, my mother walking miles to supermarkets my father used to drive her to, pulling a two-wheel aluminum shopping cart behind her. A woman feeding a family of five would not need to get supplies so often.

Despite the quirks, we had many fine get-togethers in the years immediately following my father's death. Every Saturday afternoon or evening, when Pam and I came to visit, my mother dressed up, putting on a crisply pressed matching skirt and blouse, dabbing powder on her face, and meticulously tracing two streaks of red on her otherwise pale, narrow lips. When we returned from lunch or dinner, the three of us worked on my mother's business affairs at the dining-room table, Pam painstakingly teaching my mother how to write a check so that my mother could pay her bills, something she hadn't done in thirty-eight years of marriage.

Though at first my mother made mistakes, putting down an incorrect date or penning the dollar amount on the wrong line, she eventually mastered the process, beaming as she handed Pam a completed check, which we placed in an envelope and took home with us to mail.

And though my mother usually didn't want to stray very far from her Skokie home, occasionally Pam and I persuaded her to come downtown with us to a jazz show I was reviewing. My mother resisted each of these suggestions, but whenever she did come along, she reveled in the festivities, meeting our friends, staring fascinated at the performers, soaking in the concert-hall ambience.

"Thank you for taking me out," she always said afterward, as we brought her back to the front door of her house.

"You're good kids. Now call me as soon as you get home, so I don't have to worry that something happened."

When I was out of town on assignment, Pam would take my mother to see movie matinees and out to dinner afterward. I phoned them from the road, comforted that my mother was not alone on these weekends.

Yet as the 1990s unfolded, my mother subtly began cutting back on her outings, coming up with one excuse or another why she couldn't go out to a movie or a show: the weather was going to be bad or a TV program was coming on or a phone call had to be made.

Then she started to become wary of the way Pam and I were handling her paperwork, questioning why we were placing documents in certain files and not in others.

"Tell me what you're doing with that receipt," she would say, looking over Pam's shoulder as Pam tucked away a piece of paper.

"What are you putting over there?" my mother would say to me, as if I were trying to pull a fast one while her attention had been trained on my wife.

The next week, we would come to my mother's house and find that some of the bills and receipts that we carefully had filed had been reshuffled. Initially, we thought we had blundered, putting the gas bill in the file for the water bill or misplacing a household-repair receipt. But then we began to conclude that my mother was reorganizing the works when we weren't around, though in no decipherable way.

It took time to restore order to this paperwork, and we urged my mother to leave it untouched, but she almost always responded the same way: "Never mind. I put my papers where I want." We did not understand why my mother was sabotaging our efforts, except to guess that this was simply another eccentricity of a grieving, lonely woman trying to take control of her life in the only way she could think of doing.

"I'm not going to lunch to a restaurant today—or anymore," my mother declared on the phone one Saturday morning, just before Pam and I were going to drive to her house for our weekly visit. This surprised me.

"Stop by Kaufman's Bagel Bakery on your way here and pick up some corned beef and rye bread and challah," she added. "Maybe some turkey, too. We'll eat at home."

"But wait—we always go out to lunch or dinner," I responded.

"I saw on the TV news where they showed there were bugs in the kitchen of a restaurant," my mother replied. "No more restaurants."

I tried to explain that what my mother probably saw on TV was the kind of news piece that airs every few months or so. The city of Chicago boldly trumpets that it's shutting down a restaurant, usually when inspectors find animal life there—or when the inspectors haven't been paid off by the restaurant owner *not* to find it. But to my mother, that lone TV report meant that she wasn't leaving her house to eat a meal—ever again.

Although I did not realize at the time the significance that bugs crawling in food held for my mother, it was clear that my mother's world was shrinking. Once or twice a week she took a cab to the grocery store and back; every few months she let Pam and me drive her to the bank.

And once a year, on February 16, the anniversary of my father's death, my mother returned to Rush North Shore Hospital and rode the elevator up to the third floor. She asked whoever was in charge of the nurses' station if she might be allowed to visit room 330, where my dad took his last breath. She would wait outside and, if the patient in that room happened to step out, my mother walked in and began talking to my father.

But most days and nights, she confined herself to the five rooms of her tiny Skokie home, cleaning its floors until they gleamed, conversing occasionally on the phone, and speaking to my dad, whose presence she felt.

My mother closed the door to the house, turned the key to the lock, and proceeded down the stairs toward our waiting car.

As she approached, I noticed that she was carrying something more than just the huge black purse she always had with her—there was a clear, boxlike object in her other hand. By the time she climbed into the backseat of our car, it was obvious—though hard to believe—that she was lugging a gallon of water in an unwieldy plastic jug, the Hinckley Springs label still plastered on its side.

Pam and I were dumbfounded to see this little woman, who weighed about ninety-eight pounds, lumbering under the weight of both an overstuffed purse and a gallon of water with a handle too small for anyone to hold very comfortably.

"Why are you carrying that water?" I asked, incredulously.

"Never mind," my mother said. "I might need it."

"You might need water!" I responded, with exasperation. "We're in our car! We can stop and get a glass of water or juice or a cup of coffee or anything we want, whenever we want!"

My mother was unmoved.

"Never mind," she repeated, and starting that day— sometime in the summer of 2000—my mother dragged a gallon of water with her wherever she went. To the bank, to the doctor's office, she never left home without it. To see her struggling to manage a container of water as big as her forearm—its contents sloshing back and forth as she strolled down the sidewalk—as well as a purse the size of a small suitcase was too sad to bear. We continued to beg her to leave the water at home.

When that failed, we bought her a hiker's pouch designed to hold a quart-sized plastic bottle, its black leather strap slipping easily over the shoulder. If she insisted on dragging water around, we thought, she might as well do it comfortably.

"Too small," my mother said, instantly rejecting the pouch. "A quart is not enough."

But the jug of water, alas, was just the beginning. Before long, my mother began expressing doubts about the bank where she kept her safety deposit box. On one occasion, after we went downstairs into the vault to retrieve the box, she surveyed its contents—savings bonds, jewelry, coins, keepsakes—and became agitated.

"Someone has removed some of my documents," she claimed.

"Which documents?" I asked.

"You know—house documents, bank documents," she answered. "Someone has been in this safety deposit box, someone I don't know."

We tried to explain that this was impossible—that two keys are required to open the lock guarding the box and that she held one of them—but my mother insisted that an intruder had been at work.

Moreover, when we returned home, my mother complained that someone had been inside the house while we were gone, inspecting its contents though not necessarily removing anything.

Now I started getting concerned, and once—only once—did I ask my mother if she might consider talking to a psychiatrist.

She erupted.

"You think I'm crazy—this is the kind of son I have?" she protested, her cheeks turning pink. "I raised a son to say I'm crazy? I never thought I would live to see this.

"If your father was here, he would give you such a smack in the face, you would never forget it."

The phone rang five, ten, fifteen, twenty times, and still no answer at my mother's house. I was terrified.

It was past 10 P.M. on a Tuesday night, roughly the same time that I called her every night, and I knew she would never be outside of the house at that hour.

Every five minutes I phoned, and still there was no answer. I imagined horrific scenes.

Finally I phoned the Skokie police, which agreed to send an officer. But his visit was inconclusive: my mother's house looked fine, he said; the lights were on inside, but no one seemed to be answering his knock on the door, and he didn't think the situation warranted breaking it down.

So I jumped into my car, took the thirty-minute drive to my mother's house in about half that time, and began ringing the bell and knocking on the door. No answer. Then I put my own key in the lock, turned it, and got the door open about three inches, until it was stopped by the heavy-duty chain my mother kept fastened whenever she was inside.

"Mom—are you there? Are you OK?" I shouted, as she slowly approached the door.

"Howie? Is that you?" she said, with a bit of a quaver in her voice.

"Of course it's me—let me in," I said.

She unhooked the chain and opened the door, then closed it behind me, blocking out the night.

"Someone was knocking on the door a few minutes ago—I was afraid to let them in," she said.

"It was the police," I said. "I called them, because you weren't answering your phone."

"I didn't want to answer the phone," my mother responded. "I didn't know who was calling at that hour."

I tried to explain to my mother that if she didn't answer the phone at night, she would never know who was calling, and that my sister and I immediately would worry about whether she was OK.

"Of course I'm OK," she said. "Can't you see?"

Two days later, around midnight, the ring of my own phone shattered the silence, as Pam and I slept. Oblivious, then groggy, I let that phone ring on and on before I picked it up.

I thought I heard my sister say that Mom had run out of her house and wandered the streets of Skokie before getting picked up by the police, who brought her to my Aunt Sarah's house.

Even if I had been wide awake, I would have found this tale fantastic and incomprehensible. But in the midst of sleep, it seemed an unfortunate dream. It couldn't possibly be true.

So I hung up, turned over, and continued sleeping undisturbed for hours.

When the alarm went off in the morning, I crawled out of bed, stepped into the shower, got dressed, went downstairs for breakfast, opened up the newspaper, and suddenly remembered the phone call but still didn't believe it could have been real. I continued reading.

But at my office later that day I remembered it again, and this time—finally snapping myself out of denial—I dreaded that the call might have been real, that I could not have imagined something so preposterous, even in a nightmare.

A quick phone conversation with my sister confirmed it.

"Yeah—don't you remember I called you last night?" Barb said. "Mom ran out of the house, walked in the streets, and ended up getting picked up by the Skokie police," my sister explained, adding that they drove my mother to my Aunt Sarah's house.

"She's probably there now. But I'm not sure really where she is. You better find out."

I immediately called my Aunt Sarah, who explained what happened.

"I got a call last night, past midnight, from your mother— she was at a pay phone in front of Happy Foods," my aunt said, referring to my mother's favorite grocery store, about two miles from home.

"I told her to stay there, I would call the police, and they could bring her to my house," continued my aunt.

"When she got here, your mother said that someone was in her house and that he was trying to kill her."

My aunt had told my mother that she could spend the night in one of the spare bedrooms in her house. But my mother refused to go to bed or to slip into the nightgown my aunt offered her, Sarah said. Instead, my mother sat up all night in the living room, wearing her street clothes, draped in her gray winter jacket. At her side, she stored the two brown shopping bags she had taken with her on her flight from her home, the sacks stuffed with blouses, skirts, underwear, toothbrush, toothpaste, and other essentials.

The next morning, my mother got up from Sarah's living-room sofa, combed her hair, and said she had to leave. So my aunt called for a cab to take her back home.

But by that afternoon, a separate taxi pulled into my aunt's driveway, depositing my mother there for the second time in less than twenty-four hours. My mother told Sarah that she had been back to her own house, but had decided she wasn't safe there. When my mother asked my aunt to make her a reservation at a nearby hotel, my aunt called the police instead. The officers said they were taking my mother to the emergency room of Rush North Shore Hospital, in Skokie.

"That's where I think she is now," said my aunt. "You go there and see what's going on."

Sitting up in bed in the ER at Rush North Shore Hospital, laughing robustly and gesturing broadly, speaking expansively about her life and her children, my mother looked as if she were hosting a party. The doctors and nurses who crowded around her seemed to hang on her every word, and my mother reveled in the attention.

She certainly didn't look like a woman who had been deposited there by the police just a couple of hours earlier. Smartly dressed in a black skirt and attractive blouse, her

silver hair neatly coiffed and pulled back to reveal her ani-
mated face, she practically glowed.

"Oh, Howie—I'm so glad to see you," she said. "Let me introduce you to everybody," she added, ticking off the names
of every nurse, doctor, and attendant within eyeshot, as if she
had known them for years.

"This is my son, Howard Reich—he writes for the
Chicago Tribune. Maybe you saw his articles?" she said, introducing me all around.

When the crowd finally broke up, allowing me to get
closer, I asked my mother what happened. How did she
get here? Why did she run out of her house last night, of all
things?

"I tell you what happened," she said, coolly starting to recount the tale. "Last night, my phone rang, but I didn't pick
it up. I was afraid it was that man calling.

"But then I heard his voice in the house. He said, 'I'm
going to put a bullet in your head.'"

What? I tried to recap, to see if I had understood what
she just said: "A man was in your house, and he said he was
going to do what?" I asked, unable to bring myself to repeat
her words.

"Yes, I heard him very clear. I didn't see him, but I heard
what he said: 'I'm going to put a bullet in your head.'

"So I grabbed two shopping bags, put my clothes and essentials and unmentionables inside, took some money from
my dresser drawer, and ran out of the house.

"It was past ten o'clock, I don't know exactly when. I
went to the house next door and rang the bell, but no one

answered. Then I went to the next house, and no one answered, either. Then the next one, and no one answered. No one would let me in.

"So I started walking fast down Kostner Avenue, and I heard the man's steps behind me.

"Finally, when I got to Happy Foods, on Oakton Street, I called your Aunt Sarah, and the police came to take me to her house."

My mother described in detail the appearance of the police officers, their names and ranks, the things they said to her, and the sounds she heard at night while sitting up in Aunt Sarah's living room.

The next morning, she said, she took a cab back to her house, then walked to the bank to get some more money but feared it wasn't safe to return home. So she called the Skokie police from the bank, where two officers picked her up and insisted on escorting her back home. They went into the house first, to make sure there was no intruder, then said everything was OK.

But after the police left, my mother heard a man's voice again threatening to kill her, so she ran out of the house once more—shopping bags in hand—and hopped in a cab to my Aunt Sarah's place.

"I asked Sarah to make me a reservation at a hotel to stay, but then these two men showed up who said they were police officers, and they brought me here," said my mother.

"I fought them—I told them I don't need to go to a hospital, I'm not crazy. But they threw me in here like a sack of potatoes," she said, getting agitated.

"I don't believe they were police.

"So now I'm ready to go to a hotel, so take me to one now," my mother ordered, "because I can't go home anymore. It's not safe there."

I couldn't make sense of it. My mother—who looked perfectly normal, who could recall every detail of the tumultuous past twenty-four hours—clearly was hearing voices and seeing characters who did not exist. This was many degrees beyond a woman trying to comfort herself by communing with the spirit of her long-gone husband.

I stepped out of her area in the ER and spoke to one of the doctors.

"Your mother is having some delusions, which is not so unusual among old people who live alone, but so far she has passed every neurological test," the doctor said.

"We ran MRIs on her—they were perfectly normal. We asked her what was her name, her birth date, the names of her kids, her address, the president of the United States, the date—she knows everything.

"So we want to check her into the psychiatric ward for further tests."

Sounded about right to me, but when the doctor informed my mother that she wasn't going to be checking into a hotel but, instead, into Rush North Shore's psychiatric ward, she rebelled.

"I am not crazy—I am not crazy, there is someone trying to kill me," she said, her voice rising.

"Relax, Mom," I answered. "They just want to do some more tests."

A small entourage of nurses and attendants took my mother to the building next door, where the psychiatric cases were kept in lockdown, and I met her there.

As my mother walked into her newly assigned room, unpacked her shopping bags, and put her clothes into the nightstand drawers, she fulminated.

"So you let them take me here, to the psychiatric ward," she said. "You let them lock me up.

"If your father would see this, he would beat you up so good, you never would forget it.

"I may die here, and if I do, I will come find you from the grave. When you look in the mirror, you will see me.

"You will never be rid of me."

Later that evening, Pam came to the psych ward to meet me, and my mother still raged at what she considered her imprisonment there.

"You can't keep me here—no one can keep me here if I don't want to be here," she said, launching into complaints about the meal she had been served.

"It's raw—the food they serve here is raw. And it has bugs crawling on it," she said. "I'm supposed to eat this? This is where you have put me?"

I tried to calm her.

"Mom, it's just for a short time, while we figure out what's going on—please just hold on a little while," I said.

"She's the one who put you up to this," my mother said, pointing at Pam, who lowered her head at this accusation.

We said good night to my mother, and I told her I would be back tomorrow.

As Pam and I passed through the electronic security doors, Pam asked, "Do you know what day today is?"

Well, no, I had hardly thought about it.

"February 16—the exact tenth anniversary of your father's death," Pam said. We both began to cry.

At that moment, I remembered something my mother had told me: The night before—the night she had fled the house—she had lit a candle in the kitchen, a Yahrzeit candle for my father, commemorating the date of his death, since in the Jewish tradition the day officially begins at sunset, the night before. A few moments later, she ran.

For two weeks, my mother railed about her life in the psychiatric ward, picking at food she said was uncooked, refusing to take any of the antipsychosis medication the doctors prescribed, standing aloof from the other patients and virtually everyone else.

At times she became so agitated that the nurses and orderlies had to subdue her and give her a shot of Risperdal, an age-old antipsychotic drug that slowed her down a bit but did little to improve her mental condition.

The doctors noted that my mother was somehow at once delusional yet keenly aware of her surroundings. In one report, a psychiatrist called her "a 69-year-old female who is alert and oriented times three."

"The patient tells me that after her husband died ten years ago, she heard his voice and saw his face for a short time after he died," wrote another. "She did not have any such experiences for several years until recently when occasionally he will come to her. Two days prior to admission

he told her that she should leave the house. She also received a phone call by someone threatening to 'put a bullet
in her head.'"

My mother's story never altered—she told it to doctors,
nurses, social workers, me, Pam—anyone who would listen.
She was invited to participate in group activities in the
psych ward—games, role-playing, storytelling, whatnot. In
one session, wrote a nurse in the hospital report, my mother
stayed in the room with the group "out of curiosity [and]
seemed both eager to learn new information and embar-
rassed by her lack of knowledge."

By the end of the fortnight, the doctors had reached their
diagnosis: "delusional disorder with auditory hallucinations," according to her discharge papers, which was their
way of saying that my mother had delusions and heard
voices. That much I could have told them.

We had been able to keep my mother in the psychiatric
ward on the authority of a "medical power of attorney"
document she had arranged, presciently, several years earlier. It gave my sister or me control of my mother's affairs
if a doctor determined that she was physically or mentally
incapacitated.

But on February 28, 2001, twelve days after my mother
had been admitted to the psychiatric ward, the doctors
decided that she was ready to be moved to an assisted living
facility. And if the doctors found her "capable of self care in
all areas except financial management," a psychiatrist wrote
in his assessment, I presumed they knew what they were
doing.

About five minutes after I brought my mother to Klafter Residence, an assisted living facility in the northern suburb of Wilmette, she started yelling at the people who ran it.

"You can't tell me when to take medicine," she railed, after being informed that the nurses on duty dispense meds to the residents. "This is America. I'm an American citizen," she insisted. "I decide when I take medicine, or when I don't."

It was not an auspicious beginning.

I got my mother settled into her room, a small but pleasant space with sunlight streaming in through a high, well-placed window.

The next morning I returned to check on her, and when I saw that she wasn't in her room, I walked around the premises to find her. As I approached the dining room, I saw several groups of elderly folks seated around large tables, talking and laughing. Then I spotted one woman seated alone, with about ten empty seats around her—my mother.

When I arrived at her table, she looked up and smiled radiantly at me, inviting me to sit down and asking if I wanted to try some of her fruit cocktail. I declined. We talked for awhile, then went into the living-room area and chatted some more.

Not bad, I thought. She seems a lot less distressed than in the psych ward.

Then one of the managers asked if she could speak to me alone.

"You have to tell your mother that she can't sit at the front window all day and night, looking out—it doesn't look right," the lady said.

"Also, tell her that she can't take control of the front door and decide who gets buzzed in and who doesn't. We're responsible for that.

"Please tell her, because she won't listen to us."

I knew my mother wouldn't listen to me, either, but I told her the rules, which she dismissed with a flick of her hand.

"If we don't listen to the rules," I implored my mother, "they can ask you to leave here."

"Let them," she said.

When I came to visit her a few days later, she proudly told me that she had refused to take any of the medicines that the psychiatrists had prescribed for her, and she refused to allow me to make any follow-up doctor appointments for her.

"Do you know that this place is actually a whorehouse?" my mother said to me. "Many of these women here are prostitutes. They think I'm a prostitute, too, but I am not.

"I was a married woman."

I had no idea how to respond to these comments.

She went on.

"You know, the Mystery Man keeps calling me here," she said.

"The Mystery Man?" I asked.

"Yes, the man who's going to put a bullet in my head," she explained. "I keep hearing from him."

I went home, desolate, bereft of ideas on what to do next. I called the psychiatrists who had treated my mother, and they said that if she refused to take her medication, there was nothing they could do about her delusions. I called the psych ward at Rush North Shore, and they said they couldn't re-admit her without a doctor's order.

A few days later, my mother called Pam and me to say she was moving out of the assisted-living residence—immediately! I knew that if she stepped out of that building, I might never find her again. So I begged her to stay put until I arrived, then I jumped in my car, en route calling a psychiatrist on my cell phone. He authorized another hospital visit, and several Wil-mette firefighters met me at my mother's building, forcibly taking her back to the hospital in an ambulance.

My mother seethed as she unpacked her bags. Back in Rush North Shore's psychiatric ward on March 22, 2001—three weeks after she had checked out the first time—she did not understand what was happening to her. She insisted that I, too, was wandering from one location to another, that I, too, had no home or spouse. I tried to dissuade my mother, but she seemed to be slipping more deeply into her delusions. The psychiatrists and nurses and social workers observed her, studied her, tried to talk to her, struggled to get some insight into the nightmares playing out in her waking hours.

"She presents now as she apparently is feeling threatened," wrote one of the psychiatrists in his evaluation, noting that she's "suspicious and paranoid." My mother, he added, "states that she is seeing animals and dogs chasing her." Believing these visions were real, my mother did not understand that she was suffering a mental breakdown, and therefore she refused to take any medicines. Though the hospital could inject her against her will when she became so agitated that she was a threat to herself or to others, she needed therapeutic doses of the meds—several months' worth, the doctors said—before she might even have a chance of breaking out of her psychoses. But the only way that these medications could be delivered forcibly would be if I went to court to obtain legal guardianship, and all the doctors and lawyers I consulted assured me I would lose. My mother was too alert, too aware of reality, for any judge to take away her rights.

And even if by some chance a judge agreed to, did I really want my mother to endure the trauma of forced injections daily for months on end? The thought was unbearable to me.

So as my mother continued to wander into her hallucinatory world of imagined fears merging with everyday reality, the doctors suggested I simply find a nursing home where she could be kept securely, unable to escape. There was nothing left to do, they said. Most of the nursing homes I contacted refused to accept someone with my mother's mental problems, but eventually I found a fine one not far from my home and signed her up.

I doubted my mother would voluntarily go along with the plan, but on the day I was going to move her to the new place, her reaction was worse than I expected. When I arrived in the psych ward, she was pacing the hallway, speaking loudly, gesturing with her arms, refusing to allow anyone to get near her.

"Mom, calm down—we're just taking you to another place to stay," I said.

This time, she did not greet me with her usual smile.

"Oh no, they're not taking me anywhere," she argued.

"You know where they want to take me?" she asked, without waiting for me to respond. "They want to take me to Wisconsin to work on a farm," she said.

"I heard them say it in the hallway. I hear everything they say.

"I hear them call me a dirty Jew. They say I can only sit at the table with the other dirty Jews.

"That's why they're taking me to Wisconsin—because I'm a dirty, dirty, dirty, dirty Jew."

Then my mother picked up a pay phone in the hallway, rammed in a quarter and dialed my Aunt Sarah.

"Listen to me," my mother said, nearly yelling. "They're trying to take me to Wisconsin to work on a farm or to be harmed.

"If you don't hear from me anymore, that's where I will be. Come try to find me."

In that instant—in the midst of my mother's stunning soliloquy of rage and delusion, of anger and fear and accusation—I finally, belatedly, incredibly realized that this was all about the war, and what awful things must have happened to my mother when she was a child, pursued because she was a Jew.

I now remembered that although my mother had said little about her youth, she allowed that she had been running and hiding, that she had been forced to work on farms, that she had milked cows and cleaned barns and slept in hay, that she had been fed scraps of food for her labors.

Now, through this bizarre merger of past and present, she believed that she was being sent to a farm again—not one in Eastern Europe but to the place nearest Chicago where farms are in abundance, Wisconsin. I reeled under the realization that when she had run out of her house that night a couple of months earlier, she must have been retracing events in Dubno six decades ago when she ran out of her family's home to escape the Nazis. The parallels between her childhood, which I knew so little about, and her current psychoses, which I was just starting to understand, suddenly became apparent. If in the past two months I had been preoccupied with keeping my mother off the streets and moving her from emergency rooms to psychiatric wards, now—in a sudden moment of clarity—I saw for the first time what really was happening to her.

I asked the doctors to hold off on trying to move my mother, to give me some time to try to persuade her that she was not going to be taken to a dangerous place.

Then I went home and phoned my Aunt Sarah to explain what had happened and to say that I thought I was beginning to understand that my mother's delusions were not invented but were echoes of her childhood.

And that's when my aunt belatedly told me of the conversations she had with my mother in the months before my mother fled her house.

"Your mother said there were large yellow Stars of David on her lawn," my aunt said. "I came over to her house, and she said, 'Look at what they have put on the grass.'

"I didn't know what to say. There was nothing there, except more grass.

"But your mother said there were yellow stars all over the lawn. She said, 'There's one. There's another one. And I can't get rid of them.'"

I was speechless.

On April 20, a couple weeks after my previous, failed attempt to remove my mother from the psychiatric ward, I returned to take her out of there, although she was still afraid of being taken to Wisconsin to be killed.

Once again, the nurses gave my mother a shot to calm her down. The paramedics put her in an ambulance to drive her to Glen Oaks Nursing and Rehabilitation Center, in Northbrook, while I raced ahead in my own car so that I could be there before she arrived.

I sat in the nursing home lobby for a few minutes, and then I saw my mother being wheeled into the place on a stretcher, awake and hyperaware as usual.

"Howie—how wonderful to see you," she said when she spotted me, smiling, as usual.

"I'm glad you're going to be staying here, too."

Chapter 5

CHASING THE STORY

As my mother unpacked her two brown shopping bags—carefully placing sweaters and skirts in the night-stand near her newly assigned bed—she assured me that she wouldn't be in the nursing home long.

"I have to go back to the house, to get ready to sell it," she said, a bright afternoon light streaming into the long and narrow room through half-open blinds.

"I have to get the stars off of the refrigerator and off the wall."

"What stars?" I asked, seated in a green plastic chair at the foot of her bed.

"The Stars of David," she answered. "The yellow stars."

Almost without thinking, I pulled a scrap of paper out of one pants pocket and a pen out of another and jotted down her words, verbatim. This was the first time I had ever done this. I wanted what she was saying on paper, where I could study it and try to comprehend how my mother had reached this point.

After attempting to assure her that she would be safe in the home, I told her that I would be back tomorrow, to check on how she was doing, hoping, though not believing, that her delusions might melt away, that perhaps I could help pull her back to this side of reality, where there were no Stars of David on walls and no men pointing loaded guns at her head.

But as the days and weeks unfolded, my mother continued to describe unnerving events that she believed were occurring in the nursing home, detailing them with a clarity and intensity that were difficult to argue against.

"I am told every night I am going to be killed," she said to me during one of my visits.

"They're playing bingo here, and whoever wins gets to kill me," she added.

"During the night I sleep in clothes—would you believe it?" she said, explaining that she dared not lie down on her bed, spending the dark hours seated uncomfortably in the chair alongside it.

Nor did she take showers, she said, for fear of removing her clothing, should anyone burst into her bathroom and discover her. Instead, she strategically sponge-bathed herself under her clothes.

When she stepped out of her room for meals, she said, people spat on her and called her "dirty Jew" and "kike."

There was no end to her torment, yet all the while she remained aware of the world around her. She always knew the day's date and the news of the world that played on TVs in the dining room. I had no idea how a woman who believed that the world had turned against her in such horrific ways could also converse knowledgeably about summer fires in California, news events in the Middle East, and the rising cost of gasoline.

My mother started asking me to bring her rye bread, which she said was in short supply, and when I did, she typically opened the bag immediately and voraciously devoured the first few slices. Then she put a couple of pieces in each of several plastic baggies she had asked me to bring, carefully packing the goods in a fanny pack she wore around her waist. She also stored other foods inside that bulging leather pouch—chocolates, mints, and cookies I had brought her—plus rags, toothbrush, toothpaste, soap, needle, thread, and string. Everything, I presumed, she felt she might need to have with her if she ever had to run again.

As the weeks and months passed, her appearance changed, for the worse. Unwilling to accept any of the clothes I brought to the nursing home, her sweaters and blouses became increasingly shapeless and threadbare. Her shoes—the same shoes she had hurriedly put on the night she ran out of her house—acquired layers of grime, but she refused to accept the bright white new ones I bought for her. Her hair, which was neatly coiffed when she arrived at the nursing home, became long and wiry, and she pulled it back in a ponytail, using a strand of a rag as a bow.

In a matter of just months, she transformed herself from a meticulously groomed senior citizen into someone who looked as if she had been subsisting on the margins of civilization. Yet she bragged to me that she took great pains to keep herself clean, washing her feet in a tub of warm water every day, sponging and drying the top half of her body one day, the bottom half the next. She allowed no doctor or nurse to approach her, much less examine her, and no maid to change the linens on the bed she never used.

Except for brief moments for meals outside of her room and my visits to bring her supplies and converse with her, she was alone.

The phone rang early one Saturday morning as Pam and I ate breakfast, a few months after my mother entered the nursing home.

"Your mother has escaped," said the nurse on the other end.

"What?!" I shouted.

"When she ran out, someone tried to stop her, but she fought him off," the official said. "The person went in to get help, but your mother ran away."

Exactly the thing I had dreaded had finally occurred—my mother was running again. I paced my house, desperate over this development, not knowing what to do next. Do I call the police? Do I wait for them to call? Do I begin driving the streets of Northbrook, looking for her?

Before I could gather my thoughts, the nursing home phoned again. My mother was picked up by the police, they said, and she was in the emergency room of Highland Park Hospital. I jumped in my car, raced to the ER, and again found my mother regaling the staff with stories of her latest adventure.

But this time her lip was cut, her left eye black and blue.

"I wanted to go home," she said to me. "I wanted out, and I packed up a change of clothes, underwear, everything. I slipped and fell down.

"I don't know why I slipped. I was bleeding plenty.

"But I picked myself up and kept walking. A car came by, a man came out of it, and asked if I needed help. I said 'no,' but he called 911, and an ambulance came. I don't believe they were really paramedics. They asked me to get on the stretcher, but I didn't want to go. So they put me on the stretcher and took me to the hospital."

After the doctors finished tending to my mother, I persuaded her to come into my car, so that I could bring her back to the nursing home. Apparently shaken by her flight and her fall, she didn't fight, stepping into the car and allowing me to escort her back into her room.

Back in the home, as my mother often talked about people beating her, spitting on her, trying to pull her arms out of their sockets, I took notes—constantly. She didn't seem to mind or even pay much attention. Yet if I asked her a follow-up question, she either shot down my inquiries or offered a response that left me speechless. She was nearly as wary of me as of anyone else.

"Who is trying to kill you?" I would ask, looking for specifics that might tell me more about her past and offer some way to help her.

"That's what *I'd* like to know," she would answer.

"Why are you interviewing me?" she would add. "Who sent you? Who wants to know?"

There simply was no getting to the center of my mother's reasoning, no leading from point A to point B to point C to untangle the jumble of her little-discussed past and illusory present. On rare occasions, when my mother was in a comparatively good mood, she would answer a question or two, before cutting off further conversation.

"How did you survive during the war?" I asked.

"I slept on the ground, in the snow—I ate the snow," she said. "I worked on farms. The field work was very heavy. We would dig out potatoes from the ground.

"Sometimes I stayed with people, and the man came home drunk and beat everyone up. The women had to take care of the barn, the cows, the pigs, the chickens. And then the son-of-a-gun came home drunk like a pot, and if he doesn't like what I say—pow, right in the face."

I asked my mother how she got out of Dubno and where she hid.

"Why are you investigating me?" she asked.

She refused to have a phone in her room, insisting that the "Mystery Man" who was threatening to kill her might call her again—just as he had before she fled her Skokie home. But often she was willing to talk to my sister, Barb, in Los Angeles, on my cell phone.

As soon as she heard my sister's voice, my mother began reciting her complaints, then claimed that my sister's three children had been taken away. When my sister put her kids on the phone to prove that they were alive and well, my mother argued that these weren't the same kids at all. They were children that my sister was taking care of, kids with false names, my mother said.

After hearing her make these assertions—my mother convinced to the core that she and everyone she loved was in peril—I felt powerless, depressed, unable to say much of anything. I simply sat and listened.

At the end of our visits, I would ask my mother if she would like to walk with me out of her room, to the elevator, and she always agreed, though reluctantly.

"You know, you can sleep here any night, in this bed—I never use it—and I will watch to make sure you're safe," she would say as I was preparing to leave her room.

I gently turned down the offer, and we strolled down the narrow hallway, which was bathed in institutional white light. As various nursing home residents passed us, my mother yelled at them: "Stay away from me. Don't hit me."

Then she confided, in a lowered voice, "There are a lot of people who wish me dead.

"But I have a feeling that everyone in this place is going to come out in one piece," she added, her way of saying that she and all the others would live through this ordeal.

The letter arrived in the fall of 2001, after my mother had been in the nursing home for several months.

"Dearest Sonia: I was calling you before the Holidays and as well during the Holidays several times," it began. "Unfortunately I was not able to get hold of you and also your answering machine was not in service.

"I am worried, what had happened to you; are you OK?

"Please call me."

I did not expect such a letter as I was flipping through my mother's mail, looking for bills that needed to be paid. My eyes dropped to the bottom of the page, which was signed by an Irene Tannen. I pondered the name for a few moments, then realized that the author was my mother's aunt, whom I vaguely recalled meeting in my childhood when she visited

my parents and stayed at our house for a few days. I didn't realize that my mother still had been in touch with her aunt
Irene, one of her few surviving blood relatives.

I immediately phoned Irene, told her the awful news about
my mother, and asked if I could visit her in New York, where
she worked. Several weeks after the terrorist attacks of September 11, 2001, I met Irene in a midtown Manhattan office
building where she was self-employed as a paralegal. I didn't
ask her why she still worked at age seventy-nine, enduring
the commute in and out of the city from the gated community where she lived in New Jersey.

Short, slender, and sporting closely trimmed silver hair,
Irene was hungry to hear news of my mother—though no
more than I was to find out what she could tell me about my
mother's past. Irene suggested we walk a few blocks to her favorite café, and as we wended our way through the swarm of
office workers heading home that evening, I smelled the burnt
odor of the fallen World Trade Center towers and tasted the
granular, bitter dust that still swirled through the air. A host-
ess seated us at a small table in the lounge of the Waldorf As-
toria Hotel, and I began retracing for Irene the past several
months of my mother's life. She shook her head as I offered all
the details I could remember, and I tried to answer all of her
questions.

Then it was her time to talk.

"I was never able to get the story from your mother of
what happened to her," said Irene, speaking so softly—and
looking down at the cup of tea she stirred incessantly—that
I could barely hear her.

"It was such a terrible experience. When I escaped the ghetto, my mother was still there, Zosia's mother was still there, and so was Zosia," said Irene.

Zosia, I presumed, was the Polish equivalent of my mother's name, Sonia.

"What ghetto?" I asked.

"The ghetto in Dubno—where they kept all the Jews.

"We knew we would be killed," she said, adding that some members of the family snuck out, one by one. "Later on, your mother must have escaped, too.

"It's such a painful experience, you cannot go through even talking about it."

And that was about all Irene could bring herself to say about her past, and my mother's, on that night. I didn't push her on a subject that caused her such obvious anguish. But I knew I would be back to ask for more.

"Ask Leon," Irene said to me when I returned to visit her a few weeks later.

"Who's Leon?" I said.

Irene pulled an ancient black-and-white framed photo off of an end table in her living room, an exquisitely appointed space complete with a gleaming gold Russian samovar to heat water for tea. She pointed to the little girl and boy in the embrace of a distinguished white-haired man in a suit.

"Leon is the boy," she said. "The man is his grandfather—my father—and the girl is Bluma, your mother."

"Bluma?" I said, confused. "I thought my mother was Zosia."

"Bluma was your mother's name before the war," said Irene. "Your mother became Zosia when she was hiding under false papers, and she became Sonia in the United States."

My mother had never told me this, and I pressed Irene for more.

"Bluma and Leon and his sister Fanka played together all the time in our home in Dubno. But in 1939 the Russians took over Dubno and took over our house, and we all lived in one room in the back. Your mother was maybe eight. My father lost everything and died a few months later, at age fifty-six, I believe.

"And in 1941 the Germans came in, and it got much worse."

In an instant, I remembered my mother long ago telling me that a German soldier once had grabbed her when she was a child, after she went to a place where Russian prisoners were kept. She must have told me this decades ago, and I had forgotten it until this moment. I recalled that she said the German soldier told her that he would put a bullet in her head if he ever caught her again, and I immediately blurted out this memory to Irene.

"I know exactly this story," said Irene.

"When the Germans came to Dubno, they took Russian soldiers as POWs, and they kept them not far from our home.

"And your mother and Leon's sister and everyone in Dubno saw how the soldiers were dropping and dying just from hunger. The local population thought to send children to sneak some food to them. And your mother and Leon's sister went to give some bread.

"The German caught your mother and gave her a warning: if he ever found her there again, . . . " Irene said, trailing off, unable to repeat his words.

After Irene escaped the Jewish ghetto in Dubno, she said, she lost track of my mother.

But somehow, toward the end of the war, my mother resurfaced in a farm village far outside Dubno. A friend of Irene's named Lara encountered my mother there.

"Lara said that Zosia came to her—dirty, hungry, covered with lice," recalled Irene.

"Lara was wondering how Zosia knew to find her, but Zosia somehow found out about Lara, and Zosia was in a terrible condition.

"Your mother looked horrible," continued Irene. "But Zosia and Lara couldn't acknowledge each other, because there were other people on the farm, and no one wanted anyone to know they were Jewish, or that they knew another Jew.

"This was a prevailing rule."

My mother was surviving under false papers, as a Christian, but only she knows where and how she obtained them. When Lara and my mother were finally alone for a moment, Lara took action.

"Lara washed your mother, cleaned her, stayed with her," said Irene. "And when the Ukrainians started to kill Poles at the time, Lara and Zosia escaped again, because their false identities were as Polish, and they thought they would be the next ones killed."

For the rest of the war, my mother hid in Poland with an assumed Polish identity, but my mother never told Irene what had happened to her in the years she had been hiding, nor how she survived or what she saw.

"If you want to hear more, you have to ask Leon," added Irene. "He tried to reconstruct the whole story."

I had to go to Warsaw to meet Leon, but I began to wonder how Leon might respond to hearing from me. Would he remember Sonia—or Zosia or Bluma? Would he care to talk to her son, sixty-odd years after he last saw my mother? Or would he regard me as an unwanted reminder of the worst time of his life?

As I thought through these possibilities, Irene told me that I ought to try to obtain some additional restitution payment from the German government for my mother's condition. The roughly $450 a month she had been receiving from the Germans since the 1960s as compensation for her suffering was not making much of a dent in her monthly nursing home bill of $4,000.

Irene then caught me off guard by volunteering to complete the paperwork, saying that for decades she had applied her skills as a paralegal to help Holocaust survivors obtain restitution from the German government. She never stopped working, she said, because she was afraid that if she had nothing to do all day, her bad memories might rush in and overwhelm her.

Within a few weeks, she had sent off all the forms, and a couple of months after that, the German consulate in Chicago asked me to meet with a psychiatrist they had engaged to evaluate my mother's condition.

A couple of weeks later, Dr. David Rosenberg, who was based in the northern Chicago suburb of Highland Park, met me at my mother's nursing home. A slender, mature man with dark, wavy brown hair combed straight back, he had an uncommonly intense gaze and a soothing and soft speaking voice. He asked me to wait in the lobby while he went upstairs to interview my mother. I forewarned him that their session would be less an interview and more a confrontation. He smiled and stepped into the elevator.

About twenty minutes later, he returned to the lobby and asked me to accompany him into a conference room. Then he asked me to tell him everything: what my mother was like as I was growing up, how my mother acted after the death of my father, what happened on the night my mother ran out of her house. This took about two hours. To my surprise, I wept as I told the story.

Dr. Rosenberg took notes throughout. When I asked if there was anything that could be done, he shook his head, explaining that with my mother unwilling to talk to any doctor or take any medicine, there wasn't much that he or anyone could do for her. We said good-bye, and Dr. Rosenberg told me that he would send his evaluation to the German consulate, which would forward a copy to me, while authorities in Germany decided whether my mother deserved an increase in her restitution.

A few weeks later, a copy of Dr. Rosenberg's six-page report turned up in my mailbox. I tore open the envelope and began reading the document while I was still standing in the front hallway of my house.

As painful as it was to behold, the report also brought a measure of relief. For now, in February of 2002—exactly a year after my mother fled her house—I read in scientific, authoritative detail precisely what was happening to her. Dr. Rosenberg's evaluation tracked with the deductions I had been making about my mother and her past and—this was invaluable—his analysis put a name on her condition and described it clearly, rendering the chaos of the past year a bit more comprehensible.

"When I approached her," wrote Dr. Rosenberg, referring to my mother, "she was hyperalert, quietly furious, resentful, and defensive. When I attempted to introduce myself, she stated, 'I am not talking to you or anyone. This interview is over. I am not participating. You may go now.'

"She had the inappropriate demeanor of a grand lady addressing an inferior, but her underlying appearance was of fear and mistrust," continued Dr. Rosenberg's report. "She gave the appearance of brittleness which often precedes agitation, flight or assault.

"I gently and at a respectful distance offered a proper introduction, but she rejected this, as well as offers to discuss other matters, rather than her personal information or experience. She elaborated further, 'I am not answering. You should go now.' . . . She looked like someone who might shake to pieces and sensed my presence as a dangerous intrusion."

Deeper into the document, Dr. Rosenberg made a remarkable analysis of my mother's degree of incapacity, as required by the German government. My mother, he wrote, had become virtually incapable of surviving on her own, Dr. Rosenberg concluding that she suffered "95 percent psychiatric disability for general functioning and 100 percent psychiatric disability for vocational functioning."

"The recent symptoms of wandering in the streets and the delusion that a man is going to 'put a bullet through [her] head' absolutely reproduce her traumatic experience in late childhood and early adolescence, and thus strongly document the connections between the symptoms and the National Socialist persecution," he wrote.

"Her symptoms are classic examples of the effects of deprivation from normative adolescent development; instead, she was thrust into a bizarrely hostile world and became a hunted animal, 'a jungle child,' who barely survived by the use of running, hiding and begging. . . .

"The appearance of the Star of David everywhere in her perception reproduces her fear of discovery as a Jewish child, one who never wore the emblem required by the 'Jewish Laws' of the National Socialist regime.

"Her efforts to survive during the persecution were served by hypervigilance, and by aloofness, and both of these defenses have reappeared in the last few years, but now in psychotic form and intensity. . . .

"It seems clear that Post-Traumatic Stress Disorder was the portal through which this patient entered her present psychotic state and her total state of disability."

I doubled back at these words and their force and precision in outlining my mother's illness. Yet I didn't understand how my mother could have post-traumatic stress disorder, which I then believed was something that Vietnam veterans and other soldiers came home with after their wars.

How could you live almost all of your life before getting PTSD? I phoned Dr. Rosenberg for an explanation.

"PTSD can have a late onset, too," he said. "There's an obvious connection in her condition between delayed reaction and earlier events. . . .

"Your mother is in a paranoid state. Paranoia can be disabling, but it also can be seen as an important defensive posture. Paranoia holds people together. In your mother, it is a defense posture and is reflected in the mistrust she learned in a hurry when she was on her own.

"Whether it ever went away, I doubt it.

"When it is in its full malignant blossom, my sense is that it re-emerges. . . .

"When people have tremendous trauma, like your mother, they simply never forget.

"She is in the thrall of old memories and old defenses."

Although it seems incredible to me now, every doctor who had evaluated my mother, every psychiatrist who had seen her in emergency rooms and psychiatric wards and in the nursing home had missed what Dr. Rosenberg had diagnosed. While the others had been content to slap the generic "delusional disorder" label on my mother, Dr. Rosenberg understood that my mother's past had become a veil thrown over her present.

He gave a name to what she was going through, and he identified with no doubts its source, but he also made me realize that I had much more to learn.

To my dismay, there wasn't a single book written on late-onset PTSD, nor one story in all the newspaper databases I scoured. But by interviewing PTSD specialists around the world, I was able to find what I was searching for—scientific corroboration of what I had observed in my mother's behavior and what Dr. Rosenberg had confirmed in his evaluation. A few dozen articles penned by psychiatric researchers conveyed hard data—scant but precious—about people like my mother whose traumatic childhoods had come raging back at them.

As early as 1964, a psychiatrist named William Niederland had identified an entire subset of PTSD victims—those who escaped death in the Holocaust but showed symptoms of what he coined "survivor syndrome." The survivor syndrome characteristics looked like a blueprint of my mother's problems and could include "increased arousal," "confusion between the present and the period of persecution (acting or feeling as if the traumatic event were recurring)," "psychotic and psychotic-like symptoms (illusions and hallucinations)," and "inability to verbalize the nature of the events," wrote Dr. Joel Sadavoy in a journal of psychiatry.

Moreover, "individuals with PTSD may also find themselves, or place themselves, in stressful situations, possibly to fulfill a compulsion to repeat trauma," noted Dr. Rachel Yehuda and colleagues in another journal article on the same subject.

Though the lack of widespread awareness of late-onset PTSD meant there had been a dearth of systematic studies, the few that existed contained devastating data.

In one analysis of two hundred Holocaust survivors, 85 percent showed survivor syndrome twenty to thirty years after the war, reported Sadavoy. In a 1969 study of 130 patients "who were believed to show no after-effects of the concentration camp experience," Sadavoy noted, the researcher P. Matussek "observed that, on closer inquiry, he did not see a single person in this group who was without pathology."

Most survivors had not sought psychiatric help after the war, nor were they encouraged to. The world could not bear to hear their stories, society at large making it clear to survivors that they simply should get on with their lives.

Even psychiatrists, the studies said, found the survivors' stories difficult to hear and often dissuaded patients from exploring them, helping to weave a "curtain of silence" around the subject, in the phrasing of Milton E. Jucovy in a journal of psychoanalysis. "It seemed necessary for both survivors and the external world to forget," wrote Jucovy. "Denial and repression reigned during this period of silence."

Even had the survivors sought psychiatric help, it may not have altered their fates. Because it was hard for them to trust, it was also difficult for them to put much faith in anyone else understanding their pain, many psychiatrists observed. When the survivors did attempt to explain their half-buried experiences, they often could not bear to.

Ultimately, they were caught in a trap, since the elderly inevitably look back to take stock of their pasts and assess how they have lived their lives. "The trouble is that in the process of reviewing one's life, as the memories are restored . . . and are owned up to (in other words, in the process of the return of the repressed) the individual experiences pain," wrote Dr. Henry Krystal, a pioneer in the field and a Holocaust survivor himself. Those memories, added Krystal, "are so intense, threatening and painful that one must ward them off by deadening oneself or abort the process by escaping into denial. . . .

"I have to admit that my attempts to engage aging survivors of the Holocaust in psychoanalytic psychotherapy have been for the most part unsuccessful."

Research on the subject indicated that there were many people who appeared to have led normal lives—getting married, raising children, welcoming grandchildren—before facing the delayed consequences of their devastated childhoods.

As psychiatric researchers began investigating these phenomena in the 1980s and '90s, they kept extending the length of time in which they believed a survivor could suppress the past before being overcome by it. Dr. Haim Dasberg, a PTSD expert based in Jerusalem, summed up the dawning awareness of the problem in a revelatory, unpublished paper that he emailed to me. In 1994, researcher H. Bower noticed depression and anxiety among survivors after more than three decades of latency, wrote Dasberg. Three years later, Prof. B. Schreuder observed that "it is repeatedly demonstrated to us that even after 40 years, intrusive re-experiencing is still present or has returned after years without symptoms." And in 1997, "H. Spiro et al. mentions 'numerous' case reports on delayed PTSD among POWs and ex-soldiers, even after 50 years," noted Dasberg.

My mother, however, may have beat them all, waiting fifty-six years after the war—and fully sixty-two years since the Russians invaded her "little Dubno"—until her past took hold of her present.

The PTSD analysts did more, however, than observe a new psychiatric phenomenon: they drew conclusions as to why late-onset PTSD was occurring. Essentially, Holocaust survivors were forced to fend for themselves after the war, and they rose to the challenge, putting aside—as much as was possible—the horrors of the past. They invented "what may be termed a traumatically induced 'false self,'" wrote Sadavoy, referring to "a form of character armor, protecting the victim's vulnerable true self that was impinged upon by the trauma.

"The false self meets the world successfully when supported by life circumstances such as stable marriage, having and raising children, immersion in activities and friendships, work and good health. But the traumatically affected part of the self lies vulnerable beneath the surface; emotions and thoughts are waiting to be tripped."

Other psychiatrists referred to the "splitting" between "a traumatized inner core and outward adaptation," as Dasberg put it.

Though survivors who were young and strong and preoccupied with busy lives could put their memories aside, the cumulative stress of suppressing their pasts for decades, as well as the encroaching infirmities of old age, made it increasingly difficult to continue the fight. "Ever greater amounts of energy are required to meeting ego functions," wrote Dori Laub and Nanette C. Auerhahn, "until real life becomes a fringe phenomenon around the nucleus of the trauma."

Most of the few dozen papers on the subject concurred that the devastation suffered by child survivors—77 percent of whom lost both parents—was so great that mourning was virtually impossible. For mourning was designed for loss, the natural—although difficult—cycles of life and death, not catastrophes of incomprehensible magnitude. Like parents who never can reconcile themselves to the death of a child, survivors could not easily accept or "integrate" their losses and simply move on. Their grief was "unresolved and unresolvable," in the words of Sadavoy, their only tools for dealing with it being denial, repression, and splitting.

Yet the memories, though buried deep, never really went away. They lingered, causing insomnia, nightmares, and a host of psychosomatic illnesses, from upset stomach to chronic headache. Though often "subclinical," as doctors referred to levels of anxiety that may not have been readily apparent or easily diagnosed, these symptoms gave expression to the terrifying memories that played upon the survivors' emotional stability.

Among trauma sufferers, Holocaust survivors may have been particularly vulnerable to the delayed-onset effect, for their profile was so different from soldiers in war. While Vietnam veterans with PTSD developed a "warrior syndrome" that often expressed itself in "belligerence, violence, suspiciousness, poor work history, severely disrupted interpersonal relationship, drugs and alcohol abuse, risk-taking behaviors, psychopathological disorders and self-destructive, marginal lifestyles," wrote Sadavoy, the Holocaust survivors appeared to blend in with their new worlds.

The difference, researchers believed, may have been due to the fact that veterans had faced trauma on the battlefield as uniformed combatants armed to kill, often extending their violent patterns of behavior afterward. Holocaust survivors, by contrast, were unarmed civilians who had no comparable outlet for expressing their fears and had to "resort to passive suppression of rage or other emotions," wrote Sadavoy, paraphrasing B. Goderez. After the war, the survivors continued drawing upon their already formidable strengths at tamping down their anger and shame, some earning the macabre psychiatric term "super repressors" for their ability to deny conscious awareness of their own pasts.

As I studied this material, I began conceiving it as if it were a newspaper story, which I slowly began to believe it deserved to be. For if the psychiatrists who misdiagnosed my mother didn't know all of this, if it took fully a year to encounter a few experts who did, perhaps some members of the reading public would be as startled by these discoveries as I was.

So I brought the idea to my editors, Robert Blau and George Papajohn, who ran the special projects department at the *Tribune*. They were intrigued, and Blau for particular reasons. He too was the son of Holocaust survivors, and though we had known each other for more than fifteen years, we had never discussed the subject very deeply.

"Find out more," he told me.

I would.

Among those who suffered and survived the Holocaust, none may have endured more anguish as it played out, or afterward, than children. Though only a few scientific papers touched on the particular psychological perils of PTSD among child survivors, those that did offered haunting perspectives.

"As [S.] Moskovitz (1983) discusses so poignantly, 'The loss of parents in early life means loss of the very nucleus of one's own identity,'" wrote Dr. Robert Krell, himself a child survivor, in a journal of child psychiatry. Moskovitz, continued Krell, mentions "'the continuing burden of loss the survivors feel for parents whom they have never known, a hunger for some link with the past through family connections destroyed or distorted, for traces of themselves buried in childhoods they dare not remember.'"

As I read these words, I instantly recalled my father lamenting that he hadn't saved photos of his parents and wished he could see once again what they looked like. My mother was nearly a decade younger than he and perhaps had even fainter recollections of her earliest years, before the war, and of the people who once nurtured her.

"The child survivors may have no memory [of their pre-Holocaust past]," wrote Krell. "Too young to have partaken of a foundation for life, too traumatized to experience a childhood, too preoccupied with survival to reflect on its impact, the child survivors were not blessed with the opportunity for the systematized, chronological collection of ordinary personal history."

Instead, Krell said, the children spent their formative years leading anarchic lives. They often witnessed atrocities that adults did not, because children were small and could see without being seen.

During the war, society had turned against these children, and they were left at the mercy of Christians who might save them for awhile or turn them in to authorities to be killed. Even when successfully hidden, the children's lives were turbulent, since most spent the Holocaust hiding with several different families. Because the majority of child survivors were twice orphaned, they eventually landed in adoptive families or foster homes, where they took pains to hide their pasts. For although "the elder survivor is more likely to retain a sense of pride in survivorhood," noted Krell in a journal of child psychiatry, the children felt something opposite.

"The younger survivor finds little pride and no dignity in survivorhood," wrote Krell. "As children, they experienced degradation and humiliation from their Christian neighbors, particularly other children."

So they kept quiet about their pain and shame. But even if they had railed on about it, they would have found few willing to listen. The world at large—and the scientific community in particular—was eager to assist in their denial, with some German psychiatrists, in particular, maintaining that persecuted children could not remember their pasts and therefore could not have been permanently harmed by it, wrote Milton Kestenberg and others. Kestenberg was quick to point out that even if child survivors did forget portions of their pasts, that loss inevitably represented a form of psychological damage.

But it wasn't only some German doctors who minimized their scars. "They have been told by older survivors that the children were lucky to have avoided slave labor and then live after the war in an orphanage where they were well fed and didn't have to fend for themselves," observed Sarah Moskovitz in a psychiatric journal.

In yet one more impediment to a peaceful postwar existence, the child victims did not realize the profundity of their problems. As Dasberg wrote, "child survivors have no insight or awareness of the fact that they are damaged or disordered," since they had scant frame of reference for what an ordinary childhood and adolescence looked like.

The toll of this double tragedy—psychological damage inflicted upon victims who remained unaware of it—was a constantly deepening burden of pain.

When I reported back to my editors, they were intrigued about the late-onset PTSD phenomenon but still duly skeptical about my mother.

"How do you know she doesn't have Alzheimer's disease or dementia?" Blau asked. I was ready with an answer.

Alzheimer's, I told him, is simply a form of dementia, and dementia was the farthest thing in the world from what my mother had, Dr. Rosenberg told me. "Dementia," he explained, "is a progressive loss of mental function—that is probably the best layman's definition. But dementia is first manifested by memory deficit—and there is no memory deficit with your mother at all."

On the contrary, my mother's memory proved nearly photographic. And while Alzheimer's patients struggle to learn new information, my mother's mind was picking up every name, face, and circumstance of life around her.

"Dementia would be a relief for your mother," Dr. Rosenberg said, "because then she wouldn't remember."

Furthermore, in Alzheimer's patients who develop delusions, said Dr. Rosenberg, the dementia is apparent before the delusions set in. Not so in my mother's case. Her "very advanced delusional symptoms," as Dr. Rosenberg called them, took hold of her early on, even as she showed no other mental dysfunction.

During the spring of 2003—more than two years after my mother had fled her house—I continued to bring more data to Blau and Papajohn showing that late-onset PTSD was real. They seemed persuaded, but they argued that although my story had a subject, it offered only half a narrative, since I knew virtually nothing of what happened to my mother during her childhood. The traumas at the root of her break-down remained hidden.

If I was going to write about late-onset PTSD destroying one woman's life, I needed to find the specifics of the trau-mas she suffered, the story she refused to tell. Even if I hadn't been building an article, I yearned to know specifi-cally what had happened to my mother. So my professional and personal obsessions coincided. I was convinced that I had to travel to Warsaw soon to try to find out as much as I could from my mother's cousin Leon, and then, unavoid-ably, on to Dubno, the scene of my mother's interrupted childhood.

I phoned Irene to get Leon's email address and wrote him a brief note introducing myself, explaining what happened to my mother—his cousin—and what I was trying to do.

His response came the next day: he was happy to hear from me, he wrote, noting that Irene had already told him the basics. He said that he would be happy to receive me in Warsaw, and when I phoned him a day later, he said he would be eager to travel to Dubno with me, to show me the past that he and my mother had shared.

The prospect of such a trip—which would have been un-imaginable to me a few years earlier—seemed unnervingly real now. I started having nightmares about the Holocaust, but this time the Nazis were chasing me.

On the suggestion of both Pam and Dr. Lawrence Robbins, the neurologist who had been treating me for my life-long migraine headaches, I made an appointment with an excellent psychologist. But after spending an hour telling her of my fears about this trip, I decided not to visit her again, at least not for a while. I didn't want to talk about this story, the words disappearing into thin air—I wanted to write it down.

So I began to plan the trip. I needed a *Tribune* photographer to join me, and Pam suggested a brilliant Polish lensman who had recently been hired by the paper, Zbigniew Bzdak. A short, muscular fellow with a rim of golden hair and a thick beard to match, Bzdak hardly knew who I was, having shot only one of my jazz reviews.

I found him one afternoon in the newspaper's photo lab and explained that I was working on a story that was going to take me to Poland and Ukraine.

"I go," he said enthusiastically, in his thick Polish accent, before I even told him what the expedition was all about. We made the arrangements, lining up a guide-translator and driver in Ukraine. Then I visited Blau and Papajohn one last time before heading out.

"You haven't got a story yet, you know," said Blau. I knew he was right.

Worse, I didn't even know if it was possible to piece to-gether the tale of my mother's past simply by meeting with her never-mentioned cousin in Warsaw and venturing to Dubno, the city of their birth, more than sixty years after the fact.

But if Blau's comment was meant to motivate me, it succeeded.

"I know I don't have the story," I conceded. "That's why I'm going—to get it, and I know I can," I said, half believing this.

"If you get into any problems," Papajohn chimed in, "if you get distraught about any of this, you can call me at home at any time. And, you know, you still don't have to go and do this story, if you don't feel you can. You can stop right now."

If this was his way of motivating me—editorial reverse psychology—it also worked.

"I can't stop now," I said. "I'm more afraid of backing out than of going."

A couple of weeks before venturing to Warsaw, in the summer of 2003, I flew to Los Angeles to visit my sister, Barb, her husband, Lou, and their three kids—nine-year-old Robbie, six-year-old Aaron, and three-year-old Amanda. Because I generally talked to the kids several times a week on the phone, I felt compelled to see them before my expedition into our family's past.

One afternoon, my sister and I took the kids to the park for their swimming class. As I watched them splashing gleefully in the water with dozens of other screaming youngsters, I couldn't helping thinking that whatever it was my mother suffered during the war, these three gorgeous kids would not be here—nor would my sister and me—were it not for my mother's courage and tenacity in enduring it. I teared up as my nephews and niece exulted in this blissful California afternoon, the sun glinting off the bright blue water of the swimming pool. And I marveled anew at the letter I recently had received from the German government, informing me that my mother was not ill enough to merit an increase in her restitution.

Then I remembered a haunting passage I had read a few days earlier, while organizing my research.

The nature of a child's trauma, wrote Krell, the Holocaust survivor and pioneering PTSD researcher, "raises a fundamental question. What is left when a child has everything, absolutely everything, taken away—food and nurturance, parents and grandparents, shelter and safety? And what happens if by chance that child survives? . . .

"When everything is gone, a story remains."

My parents, Sonia and Robert Reich, at a family wedding in 1956, three years after their own marriage in Chicago.

My parents with me, their first child, in the mid-1950s. We would soon be living above our bakery, in Chicago's Germantown, where the sweet scent of pastries seemed to attract everyone in the neighborhood.

Sonia and Leon played together as children in the home of their grandfather, Solomon Sys. Before the war, in the late-1930s, the children still went by their birthnames, Bluma and Leib.

Sonia's mother, Becia, as a child. After 1942, Sonia never saw her mother again.

After World War II, Irene Tannen spent months searching for her sister's children, Leon and Fanka.

My cousin, Leon Slominski (right), shortly after the war, in Ozirko, the farm village where he and his sister hid for several years.

Leon enrolled in military school after the war: "I promised myself that I never will be without a gun again."

Leon Slominski's sister, Fanka (right), with a teacher immediately after the war: "Her nervous system was wounded," said Leon.

Sonia Reich in 1946, one year
before she came to Amercia, after
most of her family had been killed.

Leon and Fanka in Gdansk, Poland, after
Fanka's graduation from pharmaceutical
school in 1963.

Leon shows me a Warsaw memorial to Polish Jews killed during the Holocaust. "Of course," said Slominski, "there were too many names to list everyone."

Leon visits the grave of his sister, Fanka, in Warsaw's historic Jewish cemetery. The gravestone lists roughly two dozen family members killed between 1939 and 1944.

Olga Chernobaj, a Ukrainian, was a girl when massacres tore apart Dubno. She described the scene for me: "From the hilltop, I saw everything."

Irene Tannen, Sonia Reich's aunt, in 2003: The war "was such a painful experience, you cannot go through even talking about it."

The remnants of the destroyed Jewish cemetery in Dubno, which has nearly returned to nature and to the animals.

Today, Lydia Dzikowska shares the old Sys family home in Dubno with two other families. Sonia and Leon spent a few years of serenity here before Dubno was invaded, in 1939.

Built in the 1500s, the central synagogue marked Dubno as possibly the oldest Jewish city in Poland. Today, the temple is used as a garbage dump.

Leon Slominski (second from right) with his family in Warsaw: His son, Peter (from left), wife Irenka, and granddaughters Katarzyna and Veronika.

As is her habit, my mother devours the bread that I bring to her in the nursing home where she now lives. Some of it she will save for later.

After scrutinizing photos that I have brought back of Dubno, my mother rejects them: "I do not want to remember this."

Chapter 6

A GLIMPSE INTO THE DARK

As I flew to Warsaw in August, Zbigniew seated next to me on a Lot Airlines jet, I imagined what my newfound cousin Leon Slominski might look like.

He would be quite short, like everyone else in my family, probably heavyset, like many men in their later years, and bald, with wisps of white hair bordering his ears. He would walk slowly, I decided, bearing the weight not only of the decades but of his childhood experiences, like my mother. And he would wear the drab, somewhat tattered clothes of a man who had spent most of his life under Soviet-style Communism.

The plane glided into its landing, and after Zbigniew and I made our way through customs at Okecie Airport, we stepped into a vast lobby where hundreds of Poles studied the faces of the arriving visitors as carefully as we studied theirs.

As I scanned the crowd, I could find no one who quite matched the image of Leon that I had envisioned. Then my eyes landed on two pieces of white computer paper, one carrying the word HOWARD, the other reading REICH. I looked upward and tried to comprehend what I saw—a tall, slender, strikingly handsome man with lucid hazel eyes, a sharply sculpted face, and impeccably cut salt-and-pepper hair. His pale blue suit jacket hadn't a single wrinkle, his off-white pants showed a crease sharp enough to cut, his brown leather shoes practically gleamed, as if they could pass military inspection.

The man looked like someone who should have been in pictures, and nothing like the cliché I had imagined. Clearly, I had a lot to learn. As I headed toward Leon, he opened his arms, a piece of computer paper still in each hand, and wrapped them around me, as if he had known me all my life and was celebrating my return.

"I am happy you are here," he said, grabbing my rolling suitcase an instant after I introduced him to Zbigniew. As Leon sailed through the airport crowd, Zbigniew and I hustled to keep pace with him, and before we knew it, our bags had been piled into the trunk of his red 2002 Citroen sedan, Leon blasting out of the parking lot at a speed that made me wish I had brought a crash helmet.

"We drop off your bags in the hotel, stop for a coffee, and then we go," said Leon, as we barreled down the highway toward central Warsaw.

After leaving our luggage at the age-old Bristol Hotel, which in an earlier era—long before the war—had been owned by the great pianist and Polish premier Ignacy Jan Paderewski, we ducked into a nearby café. Zbigniew and I, starving after our long trip, guzzled hot tea and devoured European pastries, while Leon told us his plans.

"I am going to take you to some important places, things you should see right away," Leon said, his English fluent and impressive. "I will tell you everything."

Leon insisted on paying the café bill, then we hopped back into his car and in a few minutes were standing at a marble monument. As we approached the structure—a series of walls surrounding an open-air plaza—I noticed lettering carved into its gray façade, a tableau of words without punctuation, one tumbling onto the next. Not until I stood inches away, however, did I recognize what I was looking at: hundreds of first names—Abel, Moryc, Dina, Salomon.

"These are the common names of Jews in Poland before the war, before they were killed," said Leon, only then explaining that we were standing at a Holocaust memorial.

It seemed small—a fraction of a block—considering the two million Polish Jews it was designed to commemorate.

"Of course, there were too many names to list everyone," added Leon, "so they just chose to put some of the names to represent everyone."

Then Leon walked me to a specific portion of the wall, guiding me gently by holding on to my elbow, and pointed up high at one name: Bluma.

"This is your mother's name," he said, a fact I had learned just weeks earlier.

Leon stood at the wall for quite some time, the first real pause he took since I had arrived in Warsaw.

"You know where in Warsaw we are standing?" he asked.

"No idea," I said.

"This monument is on the place where the train station stood—the Umschlagplatz—where the trains took Jews to concentration camps to be killed.

"Over there," he added, pointing to an open plot of land, "was the Jewish ghetto—the biggest in Europe, before the Nazis liquidated it and everyone inside."

I wouldn't have guessed it. Several young men and women were lying on the grass on blankets, sunbathing.

"That is not right—this is not the place for vacations," said Leon, looking away.

Then he motioned Zbigniew and me to follow him back into his car. After a short drive through town we arrived at two enormous black metal doors, parked the car, and walked into a cemetery that resembled a forest, with its immense trees rising up from amid hundreds of ornate, crumbling tombstones, some leaning over so perilously that they looked as if they might collapse at any moment.

A groundskeeper gave Leon, Zbigniew, and me black yarmulkes, which we each placed on our heads, and Leon proceeded to lead us through this city of graves, some head-stones in Hebrew, others in Polish, others so worn by time that they were difficult to read. Leon walked quickly along the winding paths like someone who had traced these steps so often that he could do it with his eyes closed.

Then he abruptly stopped at one grave, and his face—which until a moment earlier had looked so firm and strong—crumpled, a wave of emotion coming over him. He leaned toward a granite slab that lay on the ground alongside the headstone and began to brush fallen leaves off of it. Then he wet a couple of fingers on his right hand with the tip of his tongue and scrubbed a spot here and there until he was ready to explain why we had stopped, and where.

"Here I buried my sister, Fanka," Leon said softly.

"She died in 1995—she was sixty. She was very troubled after the war."

But this place was not a memorial for Leon's sister alone. The large, flat stone he had been tending to carried the names of roughly two dozen people, lined up vertically in a column beneath an inscription:

"To the memory of our closest who died and were murdered during years 1939–1944," it read.

Then came the names of the victims:

Sys Family
Solomon, Basia
Becia, Siunia,
Fritz with wife Rosa and daughter Mirka
Szapiro Family
Lejb, Sosla
Uszer, Doba
Lonia, Zhenia with husband
Seruszka with children
Kessler Family
Adolf, Jozefa

I had never heard of these men and women.

"These are the people of our family who were killed in Holocaust—almost everyone," said Leon.

"The only ones who survived were Bluma—your mother—myself, my sister, Irene, and her sister Esfir.

"The rest, killed, but we don't know how exactly.

"Only this place has their names."

We stood here for quite a while, staring at that list. I wondered what these people had looked like, how long they had lived, how much they had suffered, and why. Eventually, we left the grave, returned the yarmulkes, and stepped into Leon's car, so he could drive us back to the hotel.

"Tomorrow I tell you the story," he said.

The next afternoon, Leon returned to the hotel to recount what had happened to him and the rest of our family during the war. Zbigniew and I walked Leon past the lacquered Old World lobby of the Bristol and into its elegant lounge, gathering around a low-slung coffee table. After we ordered beverages, Leon began:

"We were together as children—your mother, my sister Fanka, and me," said Leon, recalling a moment when he was about three years old, Fanka was four or five, and my mother six or seven.

"We played in the house of our grandfather, Solomon Sys, who had a heart condition. We made so much commotion that grandfather always said, 'Put these children in separate rooms. They are too noisy together.' We made a tumult."

These rambunctious family scenes were shattered on September 17, 1939, when Soviet tanks rolled into Dubno, a couple of weeks after Germany had invaded Poland from the west, Leon said. Having signed a nonaggression pact, the Germans and Soviets effectively had divided Poland in two, with Dubno quickly becoming an occupied city.

The Soviets immediately nationalized private property, Leon explained, with Solomon Sys losing ownership of the family home, as well as his prosperous business selling hops. A few months later, Solomon Sys collapsed of a heart attack, in the spring of 1940, at age fifty-six. Family members attributed his death to the pain of losing everything he had spent a lifetime building.

"I remember well the funeral of Solomon. It was 1940; Solomon was covered in a white sheet," said Leon. "And all the way from the house to the Jewish cemetery we walked.

"And this was the beginning of the end."

Solomon's hops business had helped support everyone in the Sys family. Leon's father had worked in the business since marrying Leon's mother, who was one of Solomon Sys's daughters. At this point, Leon said he wanted to tell me that his real name was not Leon Slominski. He was born Leib Shapiro, the son of Uszer and Doba Shapiro, but like my mother and thousands of others, had assumed a new name— and a new identity—after the war.

The loss of the Sys family's property to the Russians, however, only hinted at what was to come, in 1941.

"In June the Germans entered Dubno," said Leon, just days after Hitler reneged on his unholy pact with Stalin, driving the Soviets out of Poland.

"As I remember, the soldiers of Wehrmacht, they were kind, they gave us chocolates, at first.

"But after a few days they went to the Russian front, and it got bad," added Leon, who asked to borrow my notepad and began drawing for me a map of Dubno—its main streets, the approximate location of the Sys family home, the synagogue near the center of town, so that he could illustrate his story.

"Me and my sister were standing here, maybe a block away," said Leon, pointing to a particular place on his map, "and I remember seeing an old Jewish man standing on the street.

"The old Jewish man had an armband, with a Star of David, and two young German soldiers were beating him, because he didn't take his hat off to show respect.

"I saw this."

Leon was about six years old at the time, his sister seven, he said.

A while later, though Leon didn't know exactly when, all the Sys family—Leon, Fanka, my mother, aunts, uncles, and cousins—were marched into a single room where they would live in Dubno's Jewish ghetto. And a couple of months after that, the Nazis divided the ghetto between those who could work and those who could not. Because Leon's father had managed to obtain work papers from the Germans, Leon, Fanka, and their parents were removed from the rest of the Sys family and placed elsewhere in the ghetto, and never saw my mother or most of the rest of the family again.

Sometime in 1942, Leon's flight began. As he started to recount his years as a child on the run, I imagined my mother, also a child running for her life, tracing similar steps.

"Early one morning—it was maybe a small frost—we passed through the gates of the ghetto," said Leon, explaining his family's escape. "Probably father got some knowledge that we in the ghetto will be liquidated.

"Horses were waiting, and I remember a Ukrainian man standing by them—he was nervous, and I was thinking how exciting this was and making lots of noise.

"The Ukrainian man who was sneaking us out got angry and told me, 'Don't cry—be quiet!'"

The wagon took the family to the village of Budki, about fifteen kilometers south of Dubno, where Leon and his sister and parents were dropped off with a poor Polish family named Wieczorek, Leon said.

A month later, in the winter of 1942, Leon's parents decided that the children might be less conspicuous—and have a better chance of eluding Nazis—if they were separated. So they took Fanka to the town of Malinowka, about thirty kilometers northeast of Dubno, and Leon to a village near Budki called Nowe Swiate, to a farmer named Dabrowski.

"What I remember, of course, I was crying at night, 'Where is my mother?'" said Leon.

"In the village they tried to teach me Catholic praying, just so they could say that I am not a Jew."

At that, Leon began reciting for me Catholic prayers in Polish. He smiled broadly as he delivered these words, bemused, apparently, at his ability to do this nearly six decades later. As I listened to Leon, I remembered that my mother once told me that she, too, as a child had gone to church, pretending to be Christian.

After a couple of months, in April of 1943, Leon's parents decided to risk reuniting the family, his father trekking to

Malinowka to retrieve Fanka, then bringing her and his wife to the Dabrowski farm, where Leon awaited. The Polish farmer hid the entire family in a pit in his barn. The entryway was so narrow that only one person could climb in and out at a time. When everyone was underground, Leon's father pulled over their heads a makeshift trap door covered with straw to conceal the family below. They prayed that in this ditch they might avoid Germans who were killing Jews, Ukrainians who were killing Poles, and all the rampaging across the land. Each night, the farmer Dabrowski came to the barn, opened the straw hatch, and brought the family food.

In this black pit, seven-year-old Leon, eight-year-old Fanka, and their parents stood upright—so close to one another that they could feel each other's breath—day and night for three-and-a-half months. To help pass the time, Leon's mother recited to them, in the original Russian, Aleksander Pushkin's 894-line epic poem, "The Tale of the Tsar Saltan," a narrative of a family ripped apart.

As if on cue, Leon began reciting the poem for me, its text still at the tip of his tongue.

> *Son and mother, safe and sound,*
> *Feel that they're on solid ground.*
> *From their cask, though, who will take them?*
> *Surely God will not forsake them?*

A day before Easter, in April of 1943, a group of Hungarian soldiers stormed into Nowe Swiate on horseback and set the barn ablaze—with Leon's family still inside the hole.

As Leon readied himself to continue the story, he asked if I would mind if he reverted to Polish. He simply couldn't say in English what happened next. So as Leon spoke, Zbigniew began to translate for him.

"We were still inside when the flames started, so father pushed the door open and jumped out, second was Fanka, I was third, and mother was fourth. Why fourth, I don't know.

"Anyway, mother didn't get time to go out, so she burned up. I remember hearing her crying.

"The forest was fifteen or twenty meters away, and we ran," said Leon, who, with Fanka, raced alongside his father.

"The soldiers were one hundred meters from us, and they seemed a little bit disappointed that we escaped, so they shot at us, but we covered our heads.

"I remember that father was crying that 'my wife is in there,' but they helped nothing.

"I see this picture like a photograph: the barn is in flames, soldiers in front of us, behind us the forest, and we are standing. I cannot forget this picture."

I was speechless at this. So I simply nodded my head and tried to look at Leon as gently as I could.

The three surviving members of the family, Leon said, hid in the forest, eventually attaching themselves to a couple of dozen other Jews in flight, the group perpetually running at the sight or sound of possible enemies. A few months later, in the summer of 1943, as the group sat around a daytime campfire (they dared not light one at night, for fear of being spotted), a torrent of gunshots suddenly echoed around them.

"Fanka was one hundred meters away, in a tent or some kind of shelter, and I was with father," Leon recalled.

"Then a small group of troops—five or ten men—started shooting and screaming.

"And it took one minute, or less, and all the people disappeared, dying over here or over there. I remember three or four of my known people killed in front of my eyes.

"I remember one man who got shot, and I was crying, 'Frolka, Frolka, what is wrong with you?' I couldn't understand what happened to him.

"I saw with my eyes my father was shot.

"And in this moment I was feeling that behind me there is a soldier. So I started to run, in the dirt.

"He was heavy, not so fast as me, but he was crying, 'Stop, Jew. Stop, Jew.' He was shooting at me.

"I remember the moment when I was running for my life, and with complete exhaustion I still was running.

"I fell in the dirt, from exhaustion, and one thought went through my mind: 'Why me? Why are they shooting me? I'm a good boy.'"

Leon and Fanka ran in separate directions, but somehow they found each other later, deep in the forest, eventually latching onto a few other Jews. By a staggering coincidence, one of them was a familiar face—Bronia, the widow of Leon and Fanka's uncle Siunia (a son of Solomon Sys who was killed in the Dubno ghetto). Leon and Fanka begged Bronia and the rest of the group to take them back to the site of the massacre, so the children could see if, by some miracle, their father was still alive. But as Bronia and the rest of the adults set out to look the next day, they insisted that the children stay behind.

When Bronia and the others returned, "they said, 'There were twenty or more Jewish people dead, and among them was your father,'" recalled Leon.

Amid this catastrophe, Leon and Fanka took some small solace in at least having stumbled upon Bronia, but by the winter of 1943, she and the rest of the group decided that they no longer could tend to the children while fighting for their own survival. As the weather got colder, "they realized that they didn't have much, so we understood that they wanted to leave us," said Leon.

As the hungry, haggard Jews plodded through the Polish countryside, they gradually pulled away from the children, abandoning them in the vicinity of one of the many villages where Czech farmers harvested hops that businessmen like their grandfather Solomon had sold before the war.

Leon and Fanka now were alone.

Zbigniew and I were dumbfounded by this story, and Leon's hauntingly detailed recollection of it. I shuddered to think that my mother probably had witnessed similar horrors, though, unlike Leon and Fanka—who at least had each other—my mother was on her own.

Overwhelmed by Leon's words, I asked him if we could stop for the day, to try to absorb what he had said.

He seemed relieved to take a break; his cheeks had flushed pink and a soft patina of sweat had gathered on his forehead.

So we walked him to his car, which was parked in front of the Bristol, hugged him a brief farewell, and strolled a few blocks to Warsaw's Old Town in search of relief.

We found it in a "Chopin and Jazz" concert that happened to be playing that night. As I sat in a crowded outdoor plaza—and as Zbigniew snapped photos—I basked in radiant jazz versions of Chopin's music. While pianist Filip Wojciechowski riffed on Chopin's Etude in E-flat minor, I reveled in the Impressionistic sweep and swirl of this music. And when violinist Maciej Strzelczyk found a blues undercurrent in Chopin's Prelude in E minor—the same piece that Jack Nicholson's character famously played in *Five Easy Pieces*—I felt a kind of release from the pain of Leon's story. This music breathed life back into me, as music had always done.

But at night, after Zbigniew and I returned to our rooms at the Bristol, I quickly fell into nightmares of flames engulfing me. The next morning, over breakfast, Zbigniew told me that he too had slept fitfully, visions of Leon's past roiling his dreams.

A couple of hours later, Leon was back at the hotel, seated next to me at a coffee table in the plushly appointed lounge, to finish a story I hardly could bear to hear. But there was no stopping now.

Having attended the executions of their mother and father, having been abandoned by the adults they hoped would save them—including their aunt Bronia—the children Leon and Fanka walked the dirt paths of rural Poland, looking for somewhere to rest, until they arrived in a tiny village called Ozirko. Holding hands, they stepped through muddy lanes, wandering from one farmhouse to another, until they found a barn they could slip into.

"It was deep at night; we entered the barn and went to sleep," said Leon. "And we were thinking that probably in the morning someone will come, so we will tell him what happened.

"But after morning, the midday, nobody is moving around, nobody is entering, so I went out of the barn.

"And at that moment somebody saw me, and he started to scream, picked up a pitchfork, and was running at me."

Leon and Fanka fled again, to a nearby house, where they told their story and found a more sympathetic ear. Eventually, men of the village gathered to confer on what to do with the children, who feared that this might be the end. But to Leon and Fanka's amazement, some of the farmers remembered having sold their hops to the Dubno businessmen Solomon Sys and Uszer Shapiro. If these were Sys's grandchildren, the men decided, the youngsters must be saved. One of the farmers, a twenty-four-year-old man named Vladimir Loukotka, was particularly passionate about rescuing Leon and Fanka. Loukotka, recalled Leon, had only one eye, no fingers, and one leg shorter than the other, the result of severe illness in childhood. He insisted that the village hide the children by moving them from one farm to another every day or two. In this way, Loukotka argued, the children might better avoid being spotted by marauding Germans and Ukrainians.

The strategy proved successful, and Loukotka soon decided it was safe to keep Leon on his farm and Fanka at one nearby, in the same village. Even in the embrace of these Czech families living in rural Poland, however, the possibility of execution never went away.

"Once, Ukrainian nationalists entered the village and said to the Loukotka family, 'We have to keep these children in the forest, because we don't have somebody to watch our cows, so they will be good for us,'" recalled Leon. But Loukotka realized that the Ukrainians did not really want to recruit the children simply to tend to cattle.

"Of course, it meant that they wanted just to kill us," said Leon.

To save them, Loukotka and others plied the Ukrainians with vodka until they were drunk and fed them with fresh meats until they were satiated, forgetting the children they had come to kill, Leon said.

In other instances—two or three times at least, said Leon—Loukotka and his wife were warned that Red Army troops were approaching, their reputation for rape and mayhem preceding them. So Loukotka hid his wife and Leon in a steamer trunk, leaving them inside for hours, sometimes days, until the soldiers moved on.

This was Leon and Fanka's life for the rest of the war—more than two years—and they considered themselves lucky. At least they had food and drafty barns to hide in. At least they were alive.

When the war ended, Leon said, he assumed that everyone in the Sys family had been killed. He did not know that his aunt Irene had survived and had begun to rebuild her life in Warsaw, marrying a Polish man. But while Leon and Fanka continued to live in anonymity in Ozirko in 1945 and '46, Irene listed her name and address with a Jewish cultural organization in Warsaw that tried to reconnect families. Sometime in 1946, she received a tantalizing message.

A woman at the Jewish organization, explained Leon, contacted Irene to inform her that a note had been left for her.

"There are two children of your sister Doba in a small place called Ozirko, not far from Mizoch, and they live with Volhynian Czechs," the note said.

The note was unsigned, and Leon said I needed to ask Irene what happened next.

When I returned to my room at the Bristol that evening, I phoned Irene back in the States, and she picked up the story. She told me that she eventually concluded that the only person who could have penned the note was Bronia, since she alone knew the identities of the children, where they had been left, and that Irene was their aunt. Until this note arrived, Irene had no idea that Bronia had survived, she said.

With this scant information, Irene, daring to hope that Leon and Fanka had also survived, scraped together enough money to buy a train ticket to go find them. She traveled east to the city of Rovno, which, like Dubno and other areas of eastern Poland, had been carved into a remapped Ukraine after the war, and then to Mizoch—about fifteen kilometers south of Ozirko. Desperately approaching strangers, she asked, over and over, "Did you hear of two children who were living in Ozirko during the war?"

Often the response was "Oh yes, we know them, but these two children don't want to go anywhere." And the conversation ended.

By glorious coincidence, however, Loukotka happened to be in Mizoch that day, at the market, and Irene eventually found him. He agreed to take her to Ozirko, where she saw Leon and Fanka for the first time in nearly four years. When the children realized that their aunt had come to find them, they rushed to her, but she couldn't simply whisk them away—she needed to obtain legal custody.

So she returned to Rovno, the county seat, but was told by an official, "Repatriation is closed, go to Lviv," a larger city a few hours south by train.

There Irene heard the same bad news and was instructed to travel to Kiev, the Soviet Ukrainian Republic capital; she did, but to no avail. "Repatriation is over," an official said, "but if you want to save the children, go to Moscow and do not leave there until you have the right papers, because the Soviet Union is a big country—the children eventually may be separated in different orphanages, and you will not find them again."

Irene was now out of money, so she began selling articles of clothing off her back for train fare to Moscow. There she found a group of Jews in a similar predicament, and they invited her to share their single hotel room—seventeen people in all—until she obtained the documentation needed.

Irene lived in that overcrowded hotel room for more than three months, until she received official permission to adopt Leon and Fanka, then returned to Ozirko to retrieve them. In this heroic act, she saved them from vanishing into the vastness of the Soviet Union, unconnected to anyone or anything from their past, and perhaps from one another.

But Leon and Fanka were not the same after the war.

Once Irene had brought the children to Warsaw and given them the surname of her new husband, Slominski, she saw the effects of their harrowing years of running and hiding.

Leon, at age eleven, became fixated on learning how to fire weapons and decided, against Irene's wishes, to sign up for military school.

"I promised myself that I never will be without a gun again. I will never be killed like a sitting duck," Leon told me the next day when I asked him about this.

"My loving family was made to suffer—I felt that learning to hold a gun will solve that.

"A little bit later, as a teenager, I was thinking, 'Why don't I have any good feelings about religious beliefs?' But God might not exist to a boy who saw what happened to his family."

Leon subsumed his grief and rage into a productive career in the military, where he thrived as a research scientist in radar techniques at the Technical Military Academy until Jews were booted out during a new wave of anti-Semitism in the late 1960s. He then segued into a distinguished career as a researcher at the prestigious Polish Academy of Sciences, where he received his Ph.D. degree in 1972.

His sister Fanka did not cope as well. "Her nervous system was wounded," said Leon.

After the war, he remembered, she often cried hysterically at night. She soon set about building a personal library made up almost exclusively of books about the Holocaust. She became a pharmacist but succumbed to abusing the drugs she was licensed to dispense. She periodically holed up in her apartment, unable to bring herself to go to work. All of her romantic relationships failed, including her one marriage.

Leon, by comparison, had held his life together remarkably well, having married and raised a son, Peter, who in time, gave Leon and his wife, Irenka, two gorgeous granddaughters.

But the weeklong process in which Leon toured Warsaw with me and recounted his and Fanka's story had clearly taken a toll. His huge, ready smile of a week ago was thinner and weaker, his ramrod military posture had slumped, his walking pace had slowed. A gloom had fallen over him.

"I didn't think that telling what happened would have such an effect on me, so many years later," said Leon, who lamented that he—like Zbigniew and me—was having nightmares.

He pondered my mother's mental illness and said, "I wonder if it will happen to me.

"I thought I was past this," he said. "I thought I had buried it."

But he knew he hadn't fully laid it to rest even before I came along. The Polish authorities had long since diagnosed him with survivor's syndrome, considering his heart disease, high blood pressure, and various anxieties to be rooted in his past, and because of it, the government helped pay his medical bills.

On a sunlit afternoon, a week after Zbigniew and I had arrived in Warsaw, we strolled through Warsaw's sprawling Lazienki Park. Leon, wearing white suit and tie, and his wife, Irenka, held the hands of their granddaughters, eleven-year-old Katarzyna and five-year-old Veronika. The children wore their best summer finery. As we walked the winding lanes through the park, I was not surprised to hear Leon tell me that he would not be able to proceed to Dubno with Zbigniew and me.

If the week he had spent with us had affected his health and his sleep so badly, Leon said, he did not wish to return to the place where our family was destroyed.

I grieved that I had caused Leon such troubles and that he would not come along with us. Zbigniew and I would have to go alone to the town that my mother always called, when she spoke of it, "my little Dubno."

Chapter 7

WHAT HAPPENED IN DUBNO

I DOUBTED THAT THE PROP JOB FLYING US OUT OF Warsaw would ever get off the ground. It was so puny that even Zbigniew and I, each standing barely five foot, six, had to duck our heads to get inside. Once we were in the air, the tiniest burst of wind hit the plane like a cyclone, making it impossible for me even to look at the lunch of sausage sandwiches wrapped in plastic. A couple of hours later, as we approached the ancient city of Lviv, in Ukraine, we flew so close to the treetops that I was sure our journey was going to end prematurely.

Somehow the plane landed, and we proceeded into the airport terminal, a concrete box painted dark brown. The customs officers still wore drab-green, Soviet-style military regalia—complete with red stars on their caps—and exuded menace and authority. Several studied my passport and fired questions at me, in Ukrainian. I answered "da" or "nyet" when it seemed appropriate, though I had scant idea of what they were saying (my high school Russian classes notwithstanding).

It wasn't until we got past these bulky guards and into the terminal lobby that we spotted a tall and slender, neatly dressed, fortyish Ukrainian man waving enthusiastically at us. Amid a crowd of small women wearing babushkas and mustached grandfathers with thick stubble covering their cheeks, Askold Yeremin stood out.

"Howard, Zbigniew—come, right here," he said in a thick Ukrainian accent, which I had never been happier to hear.

Via email, I had hired Askold—the national and foreign desk editor of a Lviv newspaper called the *High Castle*—to work as our guide-translator, but I had wondered if he would show up or leave us stranded in a country where we knew no one, couldn't speak a word, and didn't have a Ukrainian dime. Not only did Askold report for duty, but he brought with him an assistant from the newspaper, a rail-thin, twenty-four-year-old kid who, Askold bragged, was one of the fastest drivers in the city. Ihor Grynchyshyn, Askold enthused, had competed in many professional races, and he would be speeding us around Ukraine for the next week.

I tried to tell Askold that we might prefer a comfortable—even slow—pace, but before I could get the point across, we were in the car, rocketing past the terminal so fast that I felt as if I were back on the plane. In about two seconds, Ihor deposited us at our hotel, another chilly, Soviet-style fortress, where Zbigniew and I tossed our bags into our rooms before departing with Askold and Ihor for dinner.

The next morning, the two came to help us check out of the hotel. After a brief hassle in which the hotel clerk accused me of stealing a towel (I paid for it), we began our long drive north to Dubno.

After Lviv—a centuries-old, architecturally opulent, and incredibly cultured city—the vast rural area leading to Dubno seemed trapped in the muck of some primordial past. Decaying two-lane roads stretched for hundreds of miles, taking us past old and unsteady-looking farmhouses. Occasionally, a horse-drawn wagon laden with hay plodded along, an old man half-heartedly holding the reins.

Our driver, on the other hand, piloted his tan Daewoo sedan as if he had something to prove. But it wasn't just his astonishing speed that unnerved me, nor that whenever we hit bumps in the road, the car left the ground for a second or two before landing hard on a bump or a crater. What truly terrified Zbigniew and me was Ihor's technique for passing the other cars on the road. Choosing the worst possible moment to overtake any other vehicle, Ihor typically stepped on the gas just as we approached a hill. Each time I envisioned another car operated by a maniac just like Ihor, poised to careen through our windshield.

When there were no inclines to be found, Ihor generally preferred to pass a vehicle just as another one was bearing down on us from the opposite direction, often leaving us face-to-face with the chrome grill of a sixteen-wheeler hurtling toward the Daewoo. At the last possible instant, Ihor flicked his right wrist, steering our car out of the path of disaster, which is when Zbigniew and I usually opened our eyes. As we did, I looked to the front of our car, into Ihor's rear-view mirror, and invariably saw him smiling contentedly. Never in my soft, pampered, American life had I felt so unsafe.

After about four hours of this, we sped past a towering, totemlike structure that said "Dubno" in Cyrillic letters (finally, my high school Russian paid off). But this triumph quickly led to frustration, since Ihor didn't even tap his brakes as Dubno disappeared behind us.

"We cannot stay in a hotel in Dubno, because they do not have one," Askold told us from the front seat, a detail that I was surprised he had not bothered to mention before. "So we're driving one more hour to Rivne to find a place to stay—then we drive back," Askold said.

We checked into the decidedly no-frills Tourist Hotel in Rivne, the larger city to the north, then drove an hour back to Dubno, in the late afternoon. My heart raced when we saw that huge "Dubno" sign again, because I realized that in a few moments I would stand in the place where my mother spent her brief and interrupted childhood, the speck on the map she had called "my little Dubno" before her wartime memories of it began to consume her.

Ihor finally slowed down as we entered the village. I presumed that he didn't want to hit any pedestrians here, since we would be spending several days in Dubno and witnesses might be able to identify him. As we eased into town, I stared at its houses, squat stucco and brick structures that seemingly hadn't changed a whit since before the war, its narrow streets, and crumbling sidewalks.

Then as Ihor took a left into the city, I pulled out the Dubno map that Leon had drawn for me back in Warsaw. In a few moments, I could tell where we were: on the main commercial street of Dubno, the same road where Leon, as a child, had seen the Nazis beating an old Jewish man, the boulevard that had been called Aleksandrowicz Street for ages but was renamed Hitler Street after the Germans arrived. I asked Ihor to pull the car over so that I could walk down this avenue, to see it and feel it close up. I strolled its three or four main blocks, past age-old storefronts that my mother surely had passed as a child, until I came to the end of the road, where it split, forking on either side of a large church. Around this bend and a couple of blocks ahead, I surmised, should be the place where my mother once lived, Solomon Sys's house.

But before I got there, I noticed an immense pink building towering three stories high. This had to be the old synagogue that Leon had drawn on his map. I hurried over, Zbigniew shooting pictures all the while, Ihor and Askold following in the car. As we approached the grand edifice, which occupied about half a block, there was no question that this was the synagogue—I had seen drawings of it in history books I had examined at the library before the trip.

Battered on the outside—its paint chipped, its wood trim rotting, its foundation buttressed with weeds—the building still looked imposing, the lone architectural triumph of Dubno. I remembered from reading up on the city's history that this enormous structure was built in the late 1500s, marking Dubno as probably the oldest Jewish city in old Poland. Thousands—maybe tens of thousands—of weddings, bar mitzvahs, Sabbaths, and High Holy Days had unfolded in this magnificent place, which, inexplicably, had not been torched by the Nazis, as were most other European synagogues during the war.

As I got close to the building, which was padlocked, I peered into a narrow window and saw that the synagogue's interior had been gutted. All that remained of its innards was half a balustrade that led nowhere, hinting at a staircase where families once hustled up and down flights of stairs. The building now was cluttered with empty bottles, bags of trash, open crates, huge piles of crumpled cardboard, and other detritus.

The old synagogue of Dubno—a monument to the Jews of Poland—was a garbage dump.

Askold began asking people in the neighborhood if they knew anything about the synagogue or if any Jews were still around who could tell us about Dubno before the war. In a few minutes, we found an old man who said he belonged to the Jewish organization of Dubno. Bald, bent over, dressed in a torn undershirt and wrinkled pants, Igor Trimaskin stepped out of a tiny house about a block from the synagogue and informed us that the temple was now euphemistically being called a "recycling center." Then he appointed himself our unofficial tour guide for the day, for which I was grateful.

"I was a little boy, three or four during the war," he said.

"Too bad my mother has already died—she knew everybody here," he said to me after we told him why we were in Dubno. "She probably knew your mother."

Igor climbed into our car, saying he wanted to show us the sights. We cruised for about five minutes out of Dubno's little downtown and into a residential neighborhood, until he told the driver to stop. Then the old Jew stepped out and started walking briskly toward a small, open, overgrown gully.

"This is the Jewish cemetery," he said, leading me to believe he was crazy. There was nothing here but grass, plus the occasional goat and cow grazing on it, and a few rocks protruding from the ground.

"Look closely," Igor said, pointing at the pieces of stone, off in the distance, sprouting from the wild grass and weeds. "Those are the gravestones," he said, "or what is left of them. Probably some of your relatives are buried here."

As we walked down a steep incline to the bottom of the chasm, trying not to lose our balance, I indeed saw shards of gray rock amid the green-and-yellow foliage. I bent down to look at a piece of stone that pushed out from the earth more than any others, and I could make out a few Hebraic letters.

We spent a few minutes looking for other bits of the past—a piece of stone here, a fragment of a word there. But the place had nearly returned to nature and to the animals. After a short while, we piled back into the car, drove Igor to his little house, and sped back to Rivne.

Tomorrow, and in the days to come, I would continue to walk into my mother's past.

After breakfast the next morning, we all stepped into the car and headed back to Dubno, Ihor getting us there in a new record—for him and probably for all time—a mere forty-six minutes (I studied my watch to avoid witnessing our close encounters on the road).

Once we arrived, we went into City Hall, where we picked up a city councilman named Leonid Mosijchuk, who the day before had told us on the phone that he was Dubno's unofficial historian and could introduce us to everyone we wanted to meet. A handsome, sixty-ish man of medium height and weight with dark-brown hair slicked straight back from his forehead, Leonid was kind enough to cancel most of his appointments, so that he could guide us through Dubno's past. Askold would translate for him.

We followed Leonid's car to the home of a seventy-nine-year-old woman, Valentina Marcuk, whose grown children let us in and made pleasantries with Leonid before showing us to her bedroom, where she lay in her white nightgown. Though pale and weak, she struggled to sit up in bed to speak to us, telling us what she knew—appreciative, it seemed, that anyone wanted to hear it.

"In this area, nobody will tell you that the war began in 1941," said Marcuk, a heavyset woman with thick black-and-silver hair. "Everybody will tell you that the war began in 1939, when the Russians came," she added, referring to the infamous day of September 17, when Stalin's tanks rolled into Dubno. The previous month, Hitler and Stalin secretly had signed a nonaggression pact that effectively divided Poland between them, the Russians invading from the east less than three weeks after Germany had attacked from the west.

"There were changes, bad changes," said Marcuk. "A beautiful little Polish city became a terrible, poor Soviet city. A peaceful place became overtaken with military."

Before the Germans and the Soviets arrived, Dubno pulsed with Jewish life. Eleven synagogues, including the main one, thrived here. Klezmer bands and Yiddish theaters, Hebrew bookstores and Hassidic schools attracted Jews from Kiev, Minsk, and cities and villages farther east.

My mother was eight years old at the time, but she, Valentina Marcuk, and all the other children of Dubno— Jews and Ukrainians and Poles—now would nod to Soviet officers on the street, study Russian in school, and accept a new order of things, Marcuk said. Immediately, the Soviets dismantled the Jewish institutions of Dubno and nationalized private property. The home of Solomon Sys—where his daughters, my mother, and much of the rest of the extended family lived—became property of the Soviet government. Russian troops took over the Sys home, leaving the family to subsist in one room, in back. My mother's days of serenity had ended.

Solomon Sys—the patriarch of the family and the man my mother said she loved most in the world—collapsed of a heart attack a few months later, in the spring of 1940. Family members attributed his death, at fifty-six, to the psychological blow of losing everything he had spent a lifetime building. My mother's world, meanwhile, was coming apart before her child's eyes.

The following year, on June 22, 1941, Hitler broke his agreement with Stalin, attacking the Soviet Union, the Nazi troops reaching Dubno on June 25. More than 2,000 German and Soviet tanks clashed in and around Dubno, valuing its strategic position along the Ikva River, and Rovno, the nearby county seat (renamed Rivne after the war). Valentina Marcuk and others felt their homes tremble as mortar shells went off, she told me, bursts of fire lighting up rooms that had been darkened to avoid attack.

"It was terrible, a nightmare," said Marcuk. "Nobody could imagine that yesterday we sat at the desk at school, and today our city is barricaded by tanks on all sides.

"It was unbelievable, incredible. You could walk along the street, for example, and meet a German, and if he didn't like you, he could shoot you."

Marcuk began weeping at the memory, teetering on losing control. I told her that she didn't have to say anything else, that I appreciated what she had told me already.

"The Jews were being killed, but I can't talk any more about my impressions, because I will cry too much," she said. "I was taken and turned inside out. I became absolutely another person, and that's because I grew up with those Jewish victims. I knew them."

I stood up, shook her hand, thanked her for going through these terrible memories on my behalf, then asked Askold and Leonid if we could leave. On our way out, Leonid said that he had several more people for me to meet. As we visited their houses, a terrifying picture of what had happened in Dubno continued to emerge. Decades-old documents that I found in the Dubno Historical Museum and, later, in the United States Holocaust Memorial Museum in Washington fleshed out the story.

At exactly 4 A.M. on June 22, 1941, the first German bombs fell on Dubno, surely terrifying everyone in the Sys family home, including my mother, a ten-year-old girl.

Three days later, when the Nazis arrived, "there was a terrible panic—anyone venturing out into the street was shot on the spot," wrote survivor Yitzhak Fisher in a *Dubno Memorial Book* created by survivors after the war. (One of dozens of volumes devoted to various Jewish cities and penned in Yiddish and Hebrew, the Dubno tome traced the history of the town before, during, and after the Holocaust—a way of preserving in print what no longer existed in the flesh.)

"People began to hide," added Fisher in the *Dubno Memorial Book*. "The wheels of armored cars and tanks thundered."

The Sys family home, set back just a few feet from one of Dubno's biggest thoroughfares, must have shaken during this invasion, the windowpanes rattling, the floorboards resonating with the explosions on the streets. Once order had been restored, the Ukrainians and the Poles welcomed the Nazis with flowers, while the Jews hid in their homes, wrote Frieda Bienstock, another Dubno survivor, in the *Dubno Memorial Book*. All the while, rampant looting by the locals of Jewish stores and factories proceeded.

Worse, on this first day of the occupation, the Germans began rounding up Jews and executing them, according to a series of war-crimes reports from 1944 authored by the Soviet military and Dubno civilians after the Soviets had liberated the city. Jews immediately were machine-gunned at the old cemetery—the place where the old man Igor Trimaskin had shown me bits and pieces of headstones, the holy grounds where Solomon Sys and generations of Jews were buried.

The carnage was orchestrated by the Einsatzgruppen, the German "special action groups," mobile killing squads designed to execute as many Jews as possible in the shortest amount of time. Compared to western Poland, where Jews were sent by rail and foot to be killed in concentration camps, the methods in the east were more immediate.

In essence, Hitler considered the Soviet Union and its occupied territories to be symbols of a competing political system that had to be eradicated as quickly as possible, and the first step was the execution of its Jews. A November 1941 report by Einsatzgruppe C—the unit that streaked across Eastern Europe and directly through Dubno on its way to the infamous killings of Babi Yar, where more than 100,000 Jews were executed in Kiev—explained the rationale.

"Jews, needless to say, gave their wholehearted support to the Communists," the report said. "Under the existing conditions only one option presents itself in Volhynia [the region including Dubno]: to exterminate the Jews totally so as to eliminate conditions in which the Bolsheviks can thrive. After all, there is no doubt that they [Jews] are insignificant as a labor force, but cause great damage as carriers of the bacillus of Communism."

To provide a "legal" basis for these killings, a Nazi directive of March 13, 1941, edited by Hitler, said that in the east the "SS has been given special tasks on the orders of the Führer, in order to prepare the political administration. These tasks arise from the forthcoming final struggle of two opposing political systems. Within the framework of these tasks, the Reichsführer SS acts independently and on his own responsibility"—an explicit license to kill.

By the fourth day of the German invasion of Dubno, June 26, orders went up announcing that Jews age fourteen and older must wear a white ribbon—with a blue Star of David at its center—on the left arm, and that "a Jew caught without such a ribbon would be killed on the spot," wrote Bienstock in the *Dubno Memorial Book*. The Star of David was now synonymous with death, a lesson not lost on little Bluma. On that same day, it was announced that Jews would be given a ration of one hundred grams of bread a day, and the starvation and hoarding began.

The Germans immediately established a prison for captured Russian soldiers, located a short stroll from the Sys family home.

"We often walked by this place and gave the prisoners bread," said Iryna Polischuk, the sister of our Dubno guide Leonid Mosijchuk and, at age seventy, several years his senior. She referred to the same place where my mother and Leon's sister Fanka also had fed the starving inmates, on the day my mother was caught by the German soldier who promised that the next time he found her he would put a bullet in her head.

Every day, the situation grew worse. On July 22, Nazi SS men and Ukrainian militia began bursting into homes, seizing people, and taking them by truck to the Jewish cemetery, where large pits awaited. Now no Jew was safe at any time, any place, not even at home, their executions sometimes witnessed by the locals.

"I remember when my neighbors were taken, my girlfriend, my neighbors were taken along the street," Olga Chernobaj, a Ukrainian woman who was eight years old at the time, told me.

"I ran after them, I grabbed them.

"And the Ukrainian policeman stopped me. He was also our neighbor, and he stopped me and took my hand, and he brought me home.

"And of course my father wasn't very glad that I ran after the Jews, because he told me, 'You also could die.'"

Indeed, as the authorities rounded up Jews to take to their deaths, violence and anarchy erupted on the streets. Beatings were delivered in the open, weapons of all kinds were marshaled against the Jews and anyone standing near them. In broad daylight, "there appeared Ukrainian policemen armed with machine guns, with iron rods and with wooden staves," wrote Moshe Weisberg in the *Dubno Memorial Book*. "Some among them [wore] black masks so as not to be recognized. . . . They spread out like wild animals over the houses, yards, streets and stores, attics and cellars, dragged people from hiding places without taking pity on babies or the elderly, and poured out their wrath on those who were wounded and defenseless."

A Ukrainian policeman saved the young Olga Chernobaj from getting caught up in brutality not intended for Ukrainians like her but for Jews, pulling her out of the crowd and bringing her home. But she did not remain in her room on that August day in 1941, as her father had instructed her to do. Terrified by what she could see was happening to her friends, she snuck out of the house, she said, running as fast as she could to where her Jewish friends were being marched, to Shibennaya Hill.

She arrived at a farmhouse nearby belonging to a Ukrainian man she knew. Together they walked to the top of the ridge and watched what happened.

"From the hilltop I saw everything," Olga told me. "As we arrived, we saw that some of the Jews already lay naked and shot. At first they dug a hole, then they took off their clothes, and stood at the edge of the ground, by the hole, and they shot at them from machine guns.

"And when we came, there were only two last groups of those people who had yet to be killed. First they dug the holes, then one group took off their clothes. Then they were shot, they fell, then other people came next, and so on. And when they fell, the Ukrainian police came to the hole and covered them with something white, I don't know what it was, maybe some chemical. And then they covered them with the ground. And then the ground sometimes moved, because maybe somebody was alive.

"Some of the local people came to collect those clothes, and chose what they wanted, found some things they wanted. It was terrible."

Olga raced home and became feverish, she said. She could not sleep, she could not remain still. She was devastated too, she said, that the killings at Shibennaya Hill were done not by the Germans alone but also by the Ukrainian police. Her recollections were confirmed by the Soviet war-crimes reports, which described the massacre she had witnessed.

"This day we arrived at the excavation site, 4 km west of Dubno in the direction of the village of Kleshchikha, in the vicinity of the Shibennaya Hill, where in a gorge we discovered corpses of shot and killed peaceful people of Jewish nationality from the Dubno, Verba and Ostrozhets districts," read a report dated December 1944. "The total area of all three pits is 900 sq. m, 4 m deep," continued the report, "where there are 6,000 shot and killed people.

"During the excavation," the report continued, "it has been found that there are six to seven layers of corpses of shot people, lying with their faces down. Each layer has up to 21 rows of shot and killed people and is covered with chlorinated lime.

"The fact that the corpses are naked and lie with their faces down indicates that the shots were aimed at the back of the head and the rear area of the thorax; this is corroborated by the fact that the bullet entry hole was found in the back of the head and between the blades. The killing execution of Jewish population took place on 07.27.1941. The second time— 07.30.1941. The third execution—08.22.1941. The fourth execution—07.27.1942. The fifth execution—10.6.1942, when 3,000 people were killed. The last execution was conducted 10.24.1942; over 1,000 people were killed that day."

When the various Dubno executions were underway, "all movement into and out of the town was halted," German construction manager Herman F. Graebe said during his testimony in the Nuremberg Trials. Graebe, who had saved many Jews in Rovno, had witnessed one of the massacres in Dubno. "I saw one family of about six, all already stripped naked and waiting for the order to get down into the grave," he said at Nuremberg, of a Dubno execution in October 1942. "Next to the father was a boy of 10 or 12 years old. He placed a hand on the boy's head and pointed the other towards heaven and said something to the boy, who, I could see, was trying to keep back his tears. The man's wife was standing near an old woman with snow-white hair, either her mother or the mother of her husband, who held a baby in her arms, singing softly to it and stroking it. Then came the order, 'Next 10!' and the family started moving round the mound of earth to climb into the grave. I was standing about 10 meters away and I watched the father, the mother, the old woman with the baby, and two young girls who also belonged to the family pass by me, the boy holding his father's hand. . . .

"Then the next were called out to make themselves ready, that is, to take off their clothes. And then I heard shooting and believed that everything was over."

As this mayhem ensued, a new order on October 17, 1941, decreed that the blue Star of David on the white armband must be replaced by a yellow Star of David, to be worn on the left side of the chest and the right side of the back. With random killings, beatings, roundups, and mass executions punctuating everyday life, the stars marked the wearers as hunted prey.

Meanwhile, the cycle of roundups and executions gathered momentum. At Dubno's old airfield, "Jews, up to 5,000 men, women, old people and also children who had been shot and killed were found," the Soviet investigators noted in a war-crimes report of December 1944. "In these pits lie mainly women and children, with their heads wrapped with rags. . . . The rags are tightly wrapped several times around the mouth and nose and tied in the back with tight knots. We have counted up to 5,000 people who [have] been shot and killed or smothered to death. The killing and smothering took place on June 4, 1942, and in mid-October 1942."

A bloodbath at the Dubno airfield in October 1942 inspired one German officer who witnessed it, Capt. Axel von dem Bussche, to join a group of German officers plotting to assassinate Hitler. The plan involved Bussche blowing himself up, but, like all other attempts on Hitler's life, this one failed. Nothing—not even the heroism of Bussche, Graebe, and others like them—could save the Jews of Dubno.

At the site of the sports stadium near central Dubno, "over 3500 people were shot and killed in 50 pits," noted a report of December 25, 1944, citing executions that took place from June of 1941 to March of 1944. At the Palestine Natural Boundary, a rustic area just outside Dubno, the same report said, 1,750 people were shot and killed between the fall of 1943 and March of 1944. In a ravine near the Ikva River, "there are corpses of 575 people where on Aug. 2, 1941 shooting and killing was conducted," read a report of November 29, 1944. "During opening of the pit, the corpses were found on their knees, tilted to one side, 3–4 rows. After a group was killed, they were covered with soil, and the next round of shooting was conducted.

"When questioned, Kozlovskiy, Nikofr, a village of Zabramye resident explained that after this mass killing of Jews a stream of blood had been flowing from the ravine, whereas the Germans brought a large amount of lime and gypsum, to cover the blood. They opened the top layer of soil, poured the lime and covered it with soil, which has been confirmed during the excavation where lime and dirt mixed with gypsum was found."

Not all of the executions, however, were conducted in remote ravines and gullies. Some unfolded on the streets of Dubno.

"Often, one could hear at night, when the executions were conducted, cries of the people led to execution," said the report of November 25, 1944. "Citizen Grushetskaya, Irina, who lives across the street from the graves[,] explained that she herself had seen through her window how the Germans were leading people, day and night, in groups of ten and put them under the hill precipices, and then shot them in the back of the head. Then the corpses were covered with miscellaneous trash. Citizen Domoryeva, Yevdokya, who lives in Bozhenko St., corroborates this."

These bodies were not buried in dirt and lime, but instead were kicked down the roadsides and covered with bricks, empty cans, iron, ground beetles, bottles, and manure, typically seventy-five centimeters deep, the report said.

The war-crimes documents, which traced an ongoing series of massacres in Dubno, spared no details and proved unnerving to read. During one execution on June 4, 1942, "the Germans herded a large crowd of Jews—about 1,000 people—forced them into a pit and randomly shot them to death with submachine guns. This had been preceded by a festive reception of their guests, who were present when the women and children were being killed and were applauding festive shots," noted a report of December 1944. "A special category of German women, the so-called blitz Mädchen, were used to kill the children."

After each of these executions, the reports said, convoys of German trucks brought Dubno's citizenry to the sites to pick up the clothes and take them away. "The Germans were using 15 vehicles which had been driving back and forth during those days," said the report. Many of the Jews who hadn't yet been killed were forced to collect the clothing for the authorities, according to the accounts of survivors in the *Dubno Memorial Book*.

On March 5 and 23, 1942, thousands of Ukrainian and Polish farm wagons encircled the city, and the Ukrainian police aided the farmers in looting Jewish homes of property and food, according to the reminiscences of Moshe Weisberg and others in the *Dubno Memorial Book*. The pillaging targeted virtually every Jewish residence—including those along Panienska Street, where the Sys family lived—demonstrating to Jews that the foreign authorities, the local authorities, and much of the local populace were aligned against them. Nearly everyone was the enemy.

By the time the looting was completed and the goods placed inside the wagons, "what was left for the Jews was nothing but wrecks and broken utensils, rags and old clothes," wrote Weisberg, who sensed that the worst was yet to come, and was right.

Immediately thereafter, notices went up that the Jews would be moved into a ghetto, a nine-square-block area a quarter-mile from the Sys family home, bounded on three sides by the curve of the Ikva River, leaving its residents no escape. On the first day of Passover—April 2, 1942—Jews were to report at the site at 7 A.M. In a single day, several thousand souls proceeded into this holding pen.

"After they began to put the Jews in the ghetto in Dubno, our city became empty, quite empty," said Polischuk. High barricades went up around this instant tenement in a preexisting Dubno neighborhood, so that no one could step in or out without sanction.

"You couldn't see anything at all inside the ghetto, from the outside, because besides the iron wire that was around it, there was a high wooden fence," said Polischuk. "Some Jews were taken to work in the morning and brought back home to the ghetto at night. They wore yellow stars on their clothes.

"I saw them every day, the Jews being taken to work," Polischuk continued. "One day I saw where the cart stood, full of Jews, piled inside, one on top of another. And there were also policemen in that car.

"And one young man, he was perhaps eighteen or nineteen or twenty, in a black suit and a white shirt, he tried to jump down from that cart.

"And the policeman struck him with his gun on his head. Blood began to pour out, and all present in this car began to cry.

"I was very afraid. Later, I saw by the ghetto, near the river, three people, their heads under water, their bodies on the banks of the river."

Inside the ghetto, my mother and much of the rest of the Sys family were crowded into a single room, all sleeping on the floor, Irene had told me when I spoke to her on the phone in Warsaw. The room had no door leading outside, so they had to climb through a window to get in and out in order to obtain their daily ration of bread and to go to forced labor. As a child who was old enough to comprehend the danger of the situation—but not yet old enough to work— my mother remained in this room day and night, Irene said, the adults afraid for what might befall her on the outside. "The children were very aware of what was happening," Irene told me.

The Ukrainian militia guarded the ghetto's three gates, and Jews immediately began digging holes inside the ghetto in which to hide, creating false papers for possible future use, and otherwise trying to find ways out of this catastrophe. "It was clear that this was the end," Irene said. "We knew that we must escape from here, because everybody will be killed."

On May 15 and 16, word traveled quickly through the ghetto that huge pits were being dug outside Dubno. "Something was trembling in the air," wrote Yehoshua Vabek in the *Dubno Memorial Book*. At the same time, the ghetto population was divided into two groups: Jews who could obtain work papers and remain useful to the Nazis and to the Ukrainians were placed in one section, while Jews who could not were placed in another. In the pandemonium, Leon's branch of the family was separated from my mother's, though both wings of the family had obtained work papers.

Around midnight as May 26 became May 27, three shots were fired into the ghetto. German SS troops and Ukrainian policemen—all wearing steel helmets—stormed inside accompanied by packs of dogs, wrote Moshe Weisberg in the *Dubno Memorial Book*.

"Alle raus!" (Everyone out!), they shouted, recalled Yehoshua Vabek. "Ihr geht alle zum Tod!" (You are all going to your death), they screamed. "They started chasing the Jews from their houses and beating those who came out without mercy," wrote Weisberg. "Women fainted upon seeing their infants trampled and torn to pieces by the murderers. Those who were crippled, ill or elderly were shot on the spot."

Some mothers smothered their children, to provide a more merciful death than the Germans and Ukrainians did. Whole families jumped into the waters of the Ikva River and drowned. Those who lived through this night—which targeted those who did not have work papers—were taken to one of the massacres at Shibennaya Hill. The spectacle of the night's mayhem was branded on the survivors' memories. This is what my mother saw.

The Sys family survived this round of killings, presumably because they possessed work documents, but they realized that the next German "Aktion" would come soon. At some point, my mother stepped out of that window one last time. No one knew exactly when, and my mother never would say anything about this bleak period.

"Everybody tried to press down the memories, because you couldn't live with the memories; otherwise you could get crazy," Irene said.

Irene knew that my mother had been given false papers christening her Zosia, a classic Polish Catholic name, though Irene couldn't recall what my mother's temporary surname had been. My mother, of course, never mentioned this but had described this period of her life in only one way to me: "I was running, running, I didn't know where I was running." Through chance, heroism, divine intervention, or some combination of all of the above, she escaped the Dubno ghetto, running to farms and forests, hiding, begging, subsisting, never far from death. Often she found herself "in fields alone, and people were shooting at me," she once told my sister. Once, cowering in a thicket of wheat, she saw German soldiers beheading a woman a few feet from where she hid, she once told my sister's husband, Lou.

I don't know exactly what happened to my mother in the years she was running and hiding, an eleven-year-old girl in flight, pursued by a vast military machine. I presumed that my mother's wanderings must have been horrific, if only judging by the way I am told she looked when Lara—a friend of Irene's from Dubno—first discovered my mother on an outlying farm. Lice crawled on my mother's scalp, her clothes were dirty and torn, her fingers and feet had turned red with frostbite, Lara told Irene.

Irene did not wish to discuss in detail with me the circumstances of her reunion with my mother—she found it too upsetting to revisit. After the war, Irene said, my mother wanted only one thing in life: to leave Europe and come to America. My mother never told Irene or me exactly why, but it wasn't hard to imagine that she would want to get as far away from the death and doom of Eastern Europe, and as quickly, as possible. On May 4, 1946, the *Chicago Times* published a news article stating that "a number of Jewish survivors in Europe want to communicate with friends and relatives in Chicago." The piece, inspired by Jewish organizations trying to reconnect relatives, listed the names of several Chicago families related to European survivors, including a member of the branch of the Sys family that had lived in the States long before the war.

The Chicago family responded and helped arrange for my mother's arrival in America. On September 21, 1947, my mother stepped off the SS *Ernie Pyle* in New York, where she was greeted by an older, distant cousin. My mother was still holding most of a loaf of bread she had been too ill to eat on the ship, said the cousin, and a knife she had used to cut slices of it. Two weeks later, on October 3, my mother and two other girls arrived by train at Chicago's La Salle Street Station, the *Chicago Daily News* covering the story. "Three teen-aged Jewish war orphans from Poland met their American foster mothers today in La Salle Street Station," said the article. "They were greeted with warm smiles and a kiss by the mothers."

My mother's foster mother—her great aunt Rose Sax—gave my mother some ice cream, which my mother licked once and promptly threw up, she once told me. My mother had already changed the name she had used in hiding, Zosia, to Sophie, and eventually, upon marrying my father, she would change it again, to Sonia. Her transformation from the Polish girl Bluma to the American woman Sonia was complete; the past was finally past—until it confronted her again, sixty-odd years later.

I now knew my mother's story—what she was running from—or at least as much of it as I was ever likely to learn. Dubno, where she had begun her journey in life surrounded by love and comfort, had become a sprawling mass grave. Practically every place that I had stepped in the city had been a killing ground.

"Out of the Jewish population of 12,000," noted the war-crimes report of December 1944, "barely several dozen people had survived."

My mother, Leon, Irene, and her sister Esfira were four of them.

This knowledge overwhelmed me. Though, like many Americans, I had believed that the Holocaust was synony-mous with Jews being taken to concentration camps where millions were killed and some survived, I had no idea how differently events had unfolded in the East. Though I had heard of Babi Yar, where Germans had committed mass executions in Kiev, I had thought that this was one spectac-ular exception to the Nazis' methods. I had no idea that there were dozens—perhaps hundreds—of Babi Yars be-tween Warsaw and Moscow, and that my mother's Dubno was one of them.

A whole different Holocaust—one unmentioned when I was growing up and unexplored in the Holocaust movies and TV specials that played in America—was now staring me in the face: the Holocaust of machine guns and huge pits and thousands of bodies piled atop one another, the Holocaust of entire villages massacred. My mother had lived this Holocaust, suffered it, and survived it.

And for the first time in my life, I felt at least a fraction of what these events had meant to her. For the first time, I made emotional contact with her Holocaust, after nearly a lifetime of trying to fend it off. I realized, too, that I had been aided in my ignorance by the nature of America in the 1950s and '60s—the years of my childhood—when the subject of the Holocaust was not routinely broached in conversation. This was long before the "Holocaust" TV mini-series catapulted the narrative into American living rooms in 1978; long be-fore the massive and magnificent United States Holocaust Memorial Museum opened in Washington, D.C., in 1993;

long before Oscar-winning films such as *Schindler's List* in 1993 and *The Pianist* in 2002 made the Holocaust an incontrovertible reality in American life.

Each night for a week, when I returned to my room at the Tourist Hotel in Rivne, I splashed cold water on my face, then saw in the mirror a man facing his colossal ignorance of his mother's horrific past and his belated recognition of it. I would dab at my face with a thin towel, walk down the dark, narrow hallway, and ask Zbigniew if I could borrow the global satellite phone he had brought on the trip. I would take it back to my room, dial Pam back in Chicago, and tell her how grim it all was, without mentioning details.

At the end of the week, I was about at the limit of what I could bear to learn, and I told Pam I didn't think I could hear or see much more.

"I'm so sorry," she said. I told her I loved her, then I phoned my sister in Los Angeles, said that I was still in Eastern Europe working on a story (as always, I never had told her or anyone outside the office what story I was working on), and asked if I could talk to the kids.

Aaron, who was six, got on the phone first.

"I cut my knee today," he said, his concern over his little wound—and the characteristically raspy sound of his voice—a balm to me. "I got new sneakers, I was running around to try them out, and that's when I fell."

I assured him everything would be fine, then asked if I could talk to Robbie, who came bounding to the phone.

"How's the food over there, Uncle Howie?" said Robbie, a nine-year-old gourmand.

"Great—if you like sauerkraut," I said.

"Yuck," came the response.

At this moment, I realized—more profoundly than ever—what a miracle the mere fact of our conversation was. I brought the phone back to Zbigniew, returned to my room, took some of my migraine medicine, and collapsed on the creaky hotel-room bed, still wearing my clothes.

When I found property records identifying the location of the Sys family home, we drove to 4 Panienska Street (which was renamed Tchevchenko Street after the war). The road and the neighborhood had been weathered by the decades, but the old Sys family home was stunning to behold: standing two stories high and occupying a sprawling corner lot, it looked huge even by today's standards, dwarfing most of the houses around it. Moreover, the Sys home sat on a winding, tree-lined boulevard—one of only two Dubno streets built with fine, intricately patterned cobblestones. A huge old park stood across the street, the Ikva River flowing behind it. The location was idyllic.

"This was once the most prestigious avenue in Dubno," said Leonid Mosijchuk, the city councilman, who took us inside. "Only the rich—Jews and Poles and Ukrainians—lived on this street."

An old woman who lived there now explained that three families shared this building, which long ago had been subdivided, and she invited us in. She told us that the first people who lived in the house after the war immediately went into the cellar of the house and began digging. They had been told that Jews once lived here and had buried gold underground, hoping to reclaim it after the fighting. The Jews never returned, the woman said, and the gold was never found.

I was moved to realize that I now was standing in the place where my mother spent the years of her innocence. I lingered in the tiny room at the back of the house where the Sys family was forced to live—one person practically on top of another—after the Russians arrived. This was when my mother's first nightmare began.

Now I was ready to leave Dubno. On a bright August morning, Ihor and Askold drove Zbigniew and me back to Lviv, Askold hugged us farewell at the airport, and the next day we were showing Leon and his son, Peter, in Warsaw the pictures that Zbigniew had taken of Dubno. I couldn't bear to tell Leon most of what I had learned—he knew it all too well, anyway, from his own experiences.

But he seemed elated to see on Zbigniew's laptop the old family home in Dubno, the panoramic view of Panienska Street, even the old Aleksandrowicz Street, where he had witnessed the Jewish man being beaten by the Nazi soldier. He soaked it all in—his past and my mother's—and he enthusiastically pored over the property records I brought, documenting Solomon Sys's ownership of the family home.

"This is the first piece of paper we ever had from before the war that says our name, who we are," said Leon, studying Solomon Sys's signature, written in fountain pen with a flourish.

"We never had anything, before."

Neither had I.

Chapter 8

HEADING HOME

I SLEPT THROUGH MOST OF THE FLIGHT BACK TO CHICAGO, exhausted from the trip, the revelations, the toll of facing—for just a few days—the knowledge that my mother had been carrying with her for more than sixty years. She had experienced these events as a child, no less, and had managed to build a life despite them. I merely had heard stories about the terrors in Dubno, read documents, and witnessed the places where they had occurred, and I felt entirely depleted.

After I returned to Chicago, I was eager to spend a long visit with my mother. Though I presumed that she probably didn't want to talk about Dubno, I felt compelled to tell her about the trip—to try to let her know that I had set foot in her little hometown, that I had stood in the house where she spent a few beautiful years, that I had learned some of what had happened to her after she had fled. I brought with me photos that Zbigniew had printed out for me: images of

177

the Sys home and Panienska Street, of the synagogue and the river.

But when I arrived, my mother was fuming, practically yelling, about a recent event. As far as I could determine from talking to the staff of the nursing home, there had been a small fire on another floor of the building, causing water damage. When officials asked patients to leave their rooms so that cleanup could begin, my mother (predictably) refused. Orderlies were summoned to coax my mother out of her space and into the communal dining room, where all the patients had already gathered. But shortly after my mother got there, she snuck away from the group back to her room.

Once more, the orderlies edged her out of her room. And once more, she ran away from everyone, stealing back to her own place. Clearly no one in the nursing home realized that forcing my mother to evacuate the space in which she lived represented a replay of her wartime experiences. Until recently, I probably wouldn't have understood that, either. But even if the orderlies had perceived that they were re-enacting scenes of my mother's awful past, there likely wasn't much they could have done differently or better: the tenacity that helped save her life as a child now made her so difficult to deal with.

The third time she escaped from the group, the nurses came to her room and gave her a shot of an antipsychotic drug. Then the orderlies carried her out, still sitting in her chair, cursing them, they told me. When I came to visit, my mother was still beside herself with rage.

"They have no right to make me go," she said. "Who do they think they are? This is America!"

I tried to calm her down, to minimal effect, so I left after a short while. When I returned a couple of days later, I still had Zbigniew's pictures in hand. My mother appeared to be in a good mood, so I ventured ahead.

"I want to show you something," I said. As I opened a large manila envelope, my mother looked it over, seeming intrigued.

"I went to Dubno recently, and I saw your grandfather's house, and Panienska Street, and the Ikva River, and I wanted to show you the pictures."

My mother said nothing, but she studied the images closely, as I handed them to her, one by one. Inasmuch as I could read her face, it seemed to me that she recognized these places, perhaps because they had changed so little since her youth, perhaps because they were so deeply in-grained in her memory. She scrutinized the house on Pani-enska, the age-old Aleksandrowicz Street, the immense synagogue, the dark, muted landscape of her lost city.

As my mother gazed at these images, holding onto each picture for a few beats before moving on to the next, I told her that I had walked on these streets. I said that I had met Leon and Irene, to try to piece together the story of her past. I told her that I now knew a little bit of what happened to her during the war. But by the time my mother reached the end of the photos, she had become agitated, a stiff expression coming over her face. Though she did not deny that these images came from Dubno, and she did not dispute that I had talked to Leon and Irene, as I half expected her to, she abruptly ended my little exhibition.

"You can pack up the pictures and put them back in the envelope," she said to me sternly.

"I do not want to remember this."

I didn't make a move, however, so my mother lifted both of her arms, preparing to take a swipe at the photos, which she had placed on a table near her bed. I snatched them just before she would have hurled them to the ground. Then I put them back in the envelope, and she relaxed immediately. She began to make small talk, asking me about various relatives, indulging in her usual ritual of taking the slices of bread that I had brought her and placing them in little baggies, then stuffing the lot into her fanny pack.

We chatted for a while longer, and when I said I was ready to leave, she volunteered, as always, to escort me to the elevator. As we walked down a corridor bathed in bright fluorescent lighting, my mother as usual railed at everyone in sight. The man on the left was trying to kill her, she said. The woman on the right was planning on striking her.

Knowing what I now knew, my mother's paranoia seemed justified. Now, for the first time, I could see the terrors that she saw, for I had encountered them in Dubno, in the memories of Olga Chernobaj and Iryna Polischuk and Valentina Marcuk and in the frightening details of the war-crimes reports and the ghetto testimony.

The events that my mother was reliving were far worse than anything I could have imagined, and I grieved that they were replaying themselves in an endless loop in her

traumatized psyche. I now understood how right Dr. Rosenberg had been in evaluating my mother, when he said that
she had late-onset PTSD "with bells and whistles." By this,
I believe, he meant not only that she exhibited so many of
the classic symptoms of PTSD, including sleeplessness, hypervigilance, and intrusive recollections of past traumas.
Beyond any of these specific characteristics, my mother had
so deeply absorbed her childhood traumas into the fabric of
her being that there simply was no way she ever could escape them. Her belief that everyone was trying to kill her
and that she needed to be prepared to run at any moment
had enabled her to survive as a child and had informed her
from that point onward.

Almost as startling to me was the realization that it
wasn't only my mother who suffered PTSD. How else to explain my father's inability to sleep through the night without the help of alcohol, his perpetually recurring dreams of
machine-gunning Nazis, and his rage at the world, at the
neo-Nazis who threatened to march in Skokie, even at me?
Doctors probably would have called his symptoms "subclinical," meaning that he made his way through life, avoiding
the kind of complete breakdown that my mother eventually
suffered. Yet underneath the ebullient personality he pre-
sented to the world, he suffered greatly from the losses of his
ruined youth, and he expressed his pain in the violent out-
bursts I witnessed and experienced.

One of the PTSD studies I read concluded that no one
who survived the horrors of the Holocaust escaped its terrible imprint, every individual bearing at least some symptoms of the disorder. Though skeptics might dispute that

sweeping assessment, I needed look no further than my extended family to find supporting evidence. Their screaming
battles, cycles of feuds, and degrading ways of treating one
another made the point. They all survived an incomprehensible experience, and they continued to behave—in
ways large and small—as if it never ended. For them, it
never did.

Surveying the psychological wreckage of the war this
many years later, I couldn't help thinking of the children of
the world today—in Iraq, Israel, Gaza, the West Bank, Af-
ghanistan, Darfur, Liberia. Youngsters in these war-torn
places are suffering experiences with too many similarities
to those my mother and father endured. These children,
too, typically receive scant treatment for a disorder virtually
unrecognized by practicing psychiatrists—even if they do
end up in a place where decent psychiatric treatment might
be available.

Years from now, some of them surely will be retracing my
mother's steps, unless the world begins to realize the power
that trauma holds over the human psyche for as long as the
sufferer lives. PTSD may be the most patient and persistent
of illnesses, content to wait half a century or more to un-
leash its full wrath, when its victims are old, weak, and at
their most vulnerable.

Understanding what my mother quietly suffered as a
young adult and succumbed to in her old age, I stood newly
in awe of her heroism—unmentioned by her, to this day.
For she faced down mortal threats to her not once but twice
in her life, in her imperiled youth and again now, in the

twilight of her life. Though clearly terrified by these demons, my mother raged against them. Her undying ferocity
made me realize that, in the end, the measure of her life was
not that she had lost her grip on reality but that—through
sheer will—she had been able to hang onto it for so long,
and that even her delusions were in the service of never,
ever giving in.

I pondered these thoughts as my mother walked with me
out of her room in the nursing home on the afternoon I
showed her the pictures from Dubno. When we reached the
elevator, she hugged me gently, said she loved me, and
made her usual request.

"Don't be such a stranger," she said. "Visit more often."

A few days later, I sat down in front of the computer at
home and started working on my mother's story. I never
wrote anything as quickly in my life—five days, Monday to
Friday, to pen more than 10,000 words, starting with the
night my mother fled her house in 2001 and ending with
the moment I showed her the photos of Dubno, a few days
earlier. Occasionally I wept as I typed up passages from the
war-crimes reports, mourning those who were lost and
those, like my mother, who survived but endured their un-
seen wounds.

I filed the story to my editors the following Monday afternoon, and that evening as I prepared to go to bed, I noticed
dozens of red blotches on my skin, spread across my chest
and back. I looked as if I had been attacked by a swarm of
bees. The doctor I visited the next day said he couldn't say

exactly why this had happened, but he asked if I had been under any stress recently.

As we prepared the story for publication, one of my editors, Robert Blau, pointed out that the piece had plenty of information about my mother but little about my father. "What happened to him during the war?" Blau asked.

"He was in concentration camps," I said.

"Which ones? Where? When? What did he say about it?" asked Blau, also the son of survivors. When I told him that I didn't know, that I pretty much had tuned out my family's conversations on the subject, Blau said that I'd better find out. So I phoned a couple of my relatives, but they knew little more than I did. "Robert was in some very bad places," said one, "but who knows which ones?"

With nowhere else to turn, I headed to a bank vault and opened the safety deposit box in which I had stored my parents' papers after my mother went into the nursing home. That's where I found and read, for the first time, a sworn affidavit my father had signed on March 12, 1957, as well as a medical case history of the same period, as part of his restitution claim against the German government. The documents offered an incomplete history of my father's life from 1942 to 1945 in various concentration camps.

In Fünfteichen Concentration Camp in 1943, the documents said, he was forced to carry heavy asbestos plates and to load sand into dump cars, excruciating work that left him with lifelong back pain. As I read these words, I suddenly remembered often seeing my father holding his hands to his back, presumably trying to ease pain he did not discuss.

"Even at night we were given no rest as all types of mistreatment were ordered by the S.S. guards," he wrote. "We would sometimes be awakened and forced to march for miles, or had to submit to beatings and other types of cruelty. The conditions in Fünfteichen were so bad that 60 to 100 men died each week." At Fünfteichen, said the medical report, my father was beaten on the head until he fell down unconscious.

After two years of this, in January of 1945, my father and others were taken on a "death march" to the Buchenwald Concentration Camp. "There were about 6,000 men in this march when we left Fünfteichen, and only 200 arrived in the Buchenwald Concentration Camp, the others having died on the way," my father wrote. "The march took weeks. We were given no food and no water. It was very cold and there was snow on the ground. We were given no blankets and had to sleep out-of-doors or packed like cattle in barns. S.S. troops guarded us constantly. If a man fell he was shot to death where he had fallen."

My father was sick when he arrived at Buchenwald, he said, "but I did not report this, as I was afraid I might be sent to a crematorium. Every morning we had to stand in line for hours to be counted. The rest of the time I was forced to work within the camp at whatever the S.S. guards ordered us to do. Sometimes I was forced to throw dead bodies on to the wagons. . . . On April 11, 1945, I was liberated by the United States Army."

This was the first detailed account I had learned—the first I had opened myself up to learning—about my father's past. I was sorry that I never had asked him to tell me everything that happened. And I wished I could tell my father how much this story meant to me now.

When I told Blau what I had learned, he responded with a chilling fact: his father, too, was in Buchenwald and was also liberated from there. We were amazed to realize at this moment—after having worked on this story for more than a year and having known each other for more than fifteen— that our fathers had been in the same concentration camp at the same time.

The morning the story appeared in the Sunday *Tribune* and on its website, on November 30, 2003, emails began pouring in from around the world, but I was most concerned about the reactions of three people—Irene, Leon, and my mother. Irene told me over the phone that reading the piece reminded her that after the war she could never bring herself to ask Leon or Fanka exactly what had happened to them. The subject was too painful to broach.

"It took twenty years until I was ready to hear it," she said to me, "and even then, I asked my husband to ask them. I couldn't hear it from their lips."

Leon, speaking to me from Warsaw, said that he had been trying for decades to re-create the events that happened to the family during the war, but that none of the elders would tell him what happened to them. Whenever he brought it up, they changed the subject.

"Some things that happened," he said, "I just now read in your article for the first time."

A couple of days later I brought a copy of the piece to my mother at the nursing home and showed it to her, but she turned away.

"I don't want to see it," she said, so I put it back in the envelope.

Then she began talking about my dad.

"Sometimes in my dreams, your father talks to me," she said. "And he says, 'You are going to come out of that home and start living again and have a happy life.'"

EPILOGUE
FEBRUARY 15, 2011

FOR SEVERAL YEARS, MY MOTHER SPENT HER DAYS AND nights sitting in the plastic chair next to the unused bed in her nursing home room. This is where she slept, fully clothed, ready to run at a moment's notice. At her side, she kept a large satchel packed with underwear, toothpaste, comb, change purse—the same items she had stuffed into two brown shopping bags the night she ran out of her home in Skokie.

My struggle to learn her story pressed forward. After the article appeared in the *Tribune*, Leon told me that if I ever went back to Dubno, he would come with me for sure. A few months later, in 2004, I informed him that a documentary company in Chicago, Kartemquin Films, wanted to bring the narrative to the screen. Would Leon join me this time, as I returned to Dubno to document my mother's terrifying biography, and his?

Leon said yes, so in November the film crew and I flew to Warsaw to pick up my newfound cousin and his son, Peter, for the journey back to Dubno. When we arrived, we were relieved to discover that all the people I had interviewed for the newspaper story the year before were still alive and remembered Zbigniew and me.

Thus I would be able to interview, once again, Olga Chernobaj, the woman who had witnessed the mass killings at Shibennaya Hill when she was a child. This time, however, we would conduct the conversation not in the comfort of her Dubno living room but at the site of the executions. And Leon would be there, standing on the grounds where most of his extended family had been massacred and where he and my mother and Irene had been scheduled to die.

I cannot imagine the grief and fear that must have played on Leon's psyche as Olga described—in chilling detail—the events she saw but never could forget, wiping away tears as she spoke. As soon as her bleak soliloquy ended and before the cameras had been shut off, Leon turned away and headed back to our bus, complaining that his heart was racing and that he needed to lie down. He disappeared into his hotel room, canceling all filming for the rest of the day.

How a survivor such as Leon, or a witness such as Olga, could summon the courage to face the memory of these atrocities once again, more than half a century later, is difficult to comprehend. But I was indebted to them for telling their stories on film, for all to see.

When we finished our work in Dubno, we flew back to Warsaw, and Leon urged me to accompany him to his sister Fanka's grave in the old Jewish cemetery. Here, amid "the ghosts of our family," as Leon said, he lit a candle at the gravestone listing the names of those "whose bodies are in the fields and forests." Then Leon told me he wanted to come to the United States to visit my mother: he hadn't seen her since they were in the Dubno ghetto together, in 1942, and he thought he might be able to help her.

Months went by as we arranged the visit. Dr. Rosenberg assured me that my mother's brick-wall defenses enabled her to handle any meeting but warned that Leon "has to be prepared for a disappointment. He has to know that he might be rejected." Even so, after Leon arrived in Chicago, in the spring of 2006, he couldn't wait to get in the room to see my mother, a smile dancing across his face as he awaited my introduction.

I wasn't sure what would happen. Would my mother embrace him? Push him away? In fact, she did neither, shocking us all by refusing even to acknowledge Leon's presence. When Leon appeared in her room, my mother said, slowly and deliberately, "No—no—no—no—no." She wouldn't answer his questions, engage him in conversation, look him in the eye. Peter, who had accompanied Leon to Chicago and hoped to meet my mother for the first time, never even got into her room—things were going too badly to ask him in.

"I am crushed," Leon said in the hallway, after this disaster. "I think that this touches the core of her illness. Nothing which connects her to the past, nothing! We have nothing to do." So we left.

Though Leon had cleared several days for visiting my mother, he never saw her again.

Three years later, in 2009, my mother suffered a series of illnesses that left her less mobile and independent than before, which meant nurses could put her in bed to sleep at night and otherwise tend to her needs. Physically, she is better cared for than before. Mentally, she remains quite the same as always: hyperalert, wary, unable to separate the past from the present.

Yet, as always, she's still delighted when my sister or I come to visit. Now when I look at my mother—small, frail but defiant—I'm awed by her heroism in standing up to the horrors she believes she is facing once again.

At last, I know and love my mother for who she really is, a woman whose steadfastness as a child saved her life and eventually gave life to me and so many others, a hero who to this day wants nothing more than to live, and to protect the lives of those she loves.

Appendix:
A Guide to Resources

Because experts have only begun to study late-onset Post Traumatic Stress Disorder, research is extremely limited, most of it focusing on Holocaust survivors. Few in-depth scientific papers have been written on the subject, many unpublished.

The rest appear in arcane journals that contain tantalizing insights. Following are some of the published papers that proved most helpful. I learned of these, and many others, through the pioneering work of Haim Dasberg, M.D., a psychiatrist in Jerusalem who stands at the forefront of the field.

The Aging Survivor of the Holocaust: Integration and Self-Healing in Posttraumatic States. Krystal, Henry, M.D., (1981), Journal of Geriatric Psychiatry.

Child Survivors of the Holocaust: 40 Years Later. Krell, Robert, M.D. (July, 2005), Journal of the American Academy of Child Psychiatry. Contains several articles, including: "Introduction," Krell, Robert, M.D.; "Legal Aspects of Child Persecution During the Holocaust," Kestenberg, Milton; "A Child Survivor/Psychiatrist's Personal Adaptation," Rotenberg,

Larry, M.D.; "Role of Memories in the Lives of World War II Orphans," Hogman, Flora, Ph.D.; "Therapeutic Value of Documenting Child Survivors," Krell, Robert, M.D.; "Longitudinal Follow-up of Child Survivors of the Holocaust," Moskovitz, Sarah, Ph.D.; "Child Survivors of the Holocaust— 40 Years Later: Reflections and Commentary," Kestenberg, Judith, M.D.

Children Who Survived Japanese Concentration Camps: Clinical Observations and Therapy. Krell, Robert, M.D., (March, 1990), Canadian Journal of Psychiatry.

Demoralization and Social Supports among Holocaust Survivors. Fenig, Shmuel, M.D., and Levav, Itzhak, M.D., (March, 1991), The Journal of Nervous and Mental Disease.

Disassociation in Aging Holocaust Survivors. Yehuda, Rachel, Ph.D.; Elkin, Abbie, B.A.; Binder-Brynes, Karen, Ph.D.; Kahana, Boaz, Ph.D.; Southwick, Steven M., M.D.; Schmeidler, James, Ph.D.; Giller Jr., Earl L., M.D., Ph.D., (July, 1996), The American Journal of Psychiatry.

Do Children Cope Better Than Adults with Potentially Traumatic Stress? A 40-Year Follow-Up of Holocaust Survivors. Sigal, John J., Ph.D., and Weinfeld, Morton, Ph.D., (Spring, 2001), Psychiatry, Interpersonal and Biological Processes.

Impact of Cumulative Lifetime Trauma and Recent Stress on Current Posttraumatic Stress Disorder Symptoms in Holocaust Survivors. Yehuda, Rachel, Ph.D.; Kahana, Boaz, Ph.D.; Schmeidler, James, Ph.D.; Southwick, Steven M., M.D.; Wilson, Skye, B.A.; Giller, Earl L., M.D., Ph.D., (December, 1995), The American Journal of Psychiatry.

Impairment in Holocaust Survivors After 33 Years: Data from an Unbiased Community Sample. Eaton, William W., Ph.D.; Sigal, John J., Ph.D.; Weinfeld, Morton, Ph.D., (June, 1982), The American Journal of Psychiatry.

Knowing and Not Knowing Massive Psychic Trauma: Forms of Traumatic Memory. Laub, Dori and Auerhahn, Nanette C., (April, 1993), The International Journal of Psycho-Analysis.

Psychoanalytic Contributions to Holocaust Studies. Jucovy, Milton E., (Summer, 1992), The International Journal of Psycho-Analysis.

A Review of the Late-Life Effects of Prior Psychological Trauma. Sadavoy, Joel, M.D. (Fall, 1997), The American Journal of Geriatric Psychiatry.

Symptoms of PTSD in 124 Survivors of the Holocaust. Kuch, Klaus, M.D., and Cox, Brian J., M.A., (March 1992), The American Journal of Psychiatry.

INDEX

197